WORDSMITH

A CREATIVE WRITING COURSE FOR

YOUNG PEOPLE

FOR GRADES 7 - 9

by

Janie B. Cheaney

Published by **DGC Inc.**, Flemington, Missouri

Distributed by

See where learning takes you.

8786 Highway 21 • Melrose, FL 32666
(352) 475-5757 • Fax: (352) 475-6105
www.commonsensepress.com

Janie B. Cheaney taught her two children at home for twelve years, during which she also conducted creative writing classes for other homeschool students. Since 1990 she has seen her work published in magazines and literary journals. In addition she has worked with students in theater design and performance, and has written several plays for young people. Her first novel, *The Playmaker*, was published by Random House in 2000, followed by *The True Prince* in 2002. Mrs. Cheaney lives in the Ozarks of Missouri with her husband.

Revised 08/11
Printed 03/14

TABLE OF CONTENTS

SO YOU THINK YOU HATE WRITING

Imagine a famous painting, such as *Washington Crossing the Delaware*. The painting depicts an event that occurred long before the artist, Emmanuel Leutze, was born. Leutze had to form the picture in his head before he began the actual work--to decide on the shapes he wanted, how the forms would be arranged, and what areas of the picture would be dark or light. What you recognize as *Washington Crossing the Delaware* is the final product of many hours of thought and effort. Even for a simple composition, like the portrait known as "Whistler's Mother," the painter had hundreds of decisions to make before he ever put a brush to canvas.

An artist usually makes lots of sketches, or "studies," to determine the **composition**: the best way to arrange all the elements of the picture. Only when he is satisfied with the arrangement does he take out his brushes and start mixing paint. Even after the picture begins to take shape on canvas, the artist may discover that some of his ideas aren't working out as well as he had imagined and that changes will have to be made. Sometimes this is easy; sometimes it isn't. Sometimes an artist will abandon an incomplete painting and start over, using a completely different arrangement.

By now you may be thinking you picked up an art book by mistake. What does painting have to do with writing? Not much, on the surface. But I'm using the comparison to help you understand what writing is.

In one sense, writing is painting a picture--in words.

Let's use *Washington Crossing the Delaware* as an example. If you had stood beside the river on that icy December night in 1776, you would not have seen anything that looked like Leutze's painting. Huddled shapes scurrying silently and an occasional gleam of moonlight on a gun barrel would be all you could make out in the darkness. And if you happened to catch a glimpse of Washington himself, he would have been sitting down in the boat! But the painter had something in mind besides just recording the scene. There were dozens of boats on the water, but he chose to depict only one. On that boat he concentrated every technique, every trick of lighting and color he had learned through years of study and practice. He wanted to show the courage and determination of the Commander, the uncomplaining heroism of the "ordinary" soldiers. That one boat and its cargo have come to represent, in the minds of many, the spirit of the entire American Revolution. Quite an accomplishment for one painting!

A painter can't show everything, and a writer can't tell everything. Imagine what a job it would be to write a story that contained everything you thought and did in a single day. You could fill pages and pages but, unless you were a professional skydiver or Hollywood stunt man (and perhaps not even then), those pages would be too boring to read. It wouldn't be a story at all, just a record--with all the drama and interest of a grocery list. A writer must thoughtfully choose the elements of the story and arrange them in such a way that the reader can "see" them in the mind's eye. Instead of color, form and light, a writer has to do it all with words. It's no wonder that writing is hard work. It's hard for me, and I'm a writer!

Even if you have no plans to be a writer, you will at one time or another be asked to put your thoughts and feelings on paper. No need to panic! Writing well is hard, but it's not impossible. Just as you learned to talk early in your life, you can learn to write now. This book will teach you how to paint pictures with words. You will learn that some words "work harder" than others. Some styles succeed where others don't. Some "tricks of the trade" will help you write stronger, clearer sentences. And if you think you have nothing to write *about*, this book will make you think again. Some students may have an easier time than others expressing their thoughts on paper, but everybody has something to say.

Just as a blacksmith shapes iron and a silversmith shapes silver into objects beautiful and useful, so a wordsmith shapes our huge, bulky language into forms that make us laugh, sigh, think, or cry. That's a skill worth learning.

GET READY, GET SET . . .

If you enrolled in a painting course, you would probably spend some time in the early classes learning how to hold a brush, how to mix paint, and how to stroke the paint onto canvas. In a similar manner, Parts One and Two of this book will teach you some **techniques** of writing: how to use your tools. Part Three will give you some ideas about what to "paint," and how. No matter how accomplished a writer you believe yourself to be, it's best to start at the beginning of the book and work through to the end. Your assignments are to be written on ordinary notebook paper and *not* thrown away. Once you make a final copy of each assignment, keep it in a loose-leaf binder or portfolio.

Now that you know what to expect, think about your writing ability at this moment. Are you pretty good? Then you can use the tips included here to sharpen your skills. If you have no confidence at all, remember that you already have your supplies at hand: pencil, paper, language, and experience. This book will teach you how to use them.

PART ONE: WORD GAMES

You're starting out with one great advantage: you know English. English is an ideal language for writing because it contains so many words and offers so many different ways to put them together. For that very reason many beginning writers feel overwhelmed by the language itself and hardly know where to start. If you had a pile of 500,000 words before you, what would you do? Probably grab the words you feel most comfortable with (because you use them over and over) and arrange them in some way that sort of says what you kind of mean. But you can do better!

The first part of this book is designed to help you get a handle on words and learn how to use them effectively. You should already be familiar with verbs, nouns, adjectives and the other "parts of speech," but perhaps you could be on better terms with them. By the time you have worked through Part One, I hope you'll have some appreciation of just how wonderful and versatile these "tools" can be.

1. NAME YOUR NOUNS

Everybody learned in third grade that a noun names a person, place or thing. But did you know that there are more nouns in the English language than any other part of speech? With such a treasury of nouns, it's well worth learning how to take advantage of them.

When talking to each other we tend to be lazy, saying,

"Put that over there,"

When we could say,

"Put the crystal vase on the mantle," or,

"Put the lace tablecloth on the dining room table," or

"Put the cat in the dishwasher."

But writers can't be lazy. Look at this paragraph:

```
     Last Saturday I saw two men get into an
argument at the park.  The first man raised his
voice.  The second man asked a question and the
first man got even angrier.  The second man laughed,
but it didn't sound like a happy laugh.  The first
man rolled up his newspaper and I thought he was
going to hit the second man over the head with it!
Instead he hit his own hand....
```

And so on. Does "first man," "second man," back and forth, seem a little repetitious to you? "First" and "second" are words that tell us nothing *about* these two men. Perhaps we could give them a little personality:

```
     Last Saturday I saw two men get into an
argument at St. Francis Park.  One was rather stout,
wore a business suit, and carried a newspaper.  The
other was dressed in a greasy khaki uniform, like an
auto mechanic.  The stout man raised his voice.  The
other asked a question, which seemed to make the
businessman even angrier.  The mechanic laughed, but
it didn't sound like a happy laugh.  Mr. Businessman
rolled up his newspaper and I thought he was going
to hit his opponent over the head!  Instead he
brought the newspaper down on his own palm....
```

Naming the park gives us a sense of being in a real place, not just any park. Dressing the two men in distinctive clothes helps us to identify them. Business suits are a type of "uniform," like the khaki work clothes; a suit does not necessarily make a businessman, but that's how most men, so dressed, would first appear to us. But

WORDSMITH - PART ONE

"mechanic" and "businessman," though handy labels, could become just as tiresome as "first man" and "second man." I came up with another name for Man #2: "his opponent." Not only does this word provide another label to use, but it also helps us define the relationship between the two characters.

Finally, notice that I changed "hand" to "palm" in the next-to-last sentence. The palm, as you know, is a part of the hand. You might hit your *hand* by accident, or as a humorous way of saying, "naughty, naughty" to yourself. But you would hit your *palm,* with a fist or ruler or rolled-up newspaper, to make a point or to show that you mean business. Try it yourself. Pick up your pencil and strike your knuckles, then the back of your hand, then your palm. Doesn't each of these actions send a different message? (Is anyone looking at you as though you'd lost your mind?)

By changing a few nouns and adding some details, I bring the picture of these two men into much sharper focus. Who's the more aggressive? What tells you the mechanic may be down on his luck? Who will probably win this argument?

In each case, the noun we substituted was more **concrete** than the original. Concrete is solid and specific as opposed to general and abstract. Concrete nouns build a firm foundation for your writing.

✍**EXERCISE 1-A.** Below is a list of general nouns. By "general," I mean that these nouns can cover a broad area, like a corral. Inside a cattle corral you might find cows, calves, Herefords, and Jerseys. A car corral might contain vans, convertibles, Chevys, Hondas and Jaguars. In the body corral we find noses, arms, toes and hips.

Write at least five concrete nouns for each general noun in the following list. The first one is done for you:

man *father, painter, teacher, official, player* _____

ball _____

tree _____

cup _____

dish _____

dog _____

street _____

day _____

bed (or anything to lie on) _____

_____

3

chair (or anything to sit on) _____

_____

✍EXERCISE 1-B.   For each of the sentences below, write three more sentences, substituting specific nouns for the underlined words. Then add another sentence or phrase to tell what happened next. In each of the examples below, notice how a concrete noun changes the whole scenario. A "tractor" roaring up a "downtown boulevard" will produce different results from a "Porsche" roaring up a "suburban cul-de-sac," as your additional phrase or sentence should demonstrate.

> **EXAMPLE:** John stopped the ball with his body.
>
> John stopped the soccer ball with his hip. As it bounced away, he charged after it.
>
> John stopped the golf ball with his foot. "You're putting out of turn," he snapped.
>
> John stopped the baseball with his head, then crumpled to the ground.

1.   The car roared up the street.

1a. _____

_____

_____

1b. _____

_____

_____

1c. _____

_____

_____

2.   The man walked his dog down Cherry Lane each morning.

2a. _____

_____

_____

2b. _____

_____

_____

2b. _____

_____

_____

3. She put the <u>flowers</u> in a <u>dish</u> on the table.

3a. _____

_____

_____

3b. _____

_____

_____

3c. _____

_____

_____

4. Henry sat in the <u>chair</u> they showed him.

4a. _____

_____

_____

4b. _____

_____

_____

4c. _____

_____

_____

5. Mr. Pierce was lying on a <u>bed</u> as we entered.

5a. _____

_____

_____

5b. _____

_____

_____

5c. _____

_____

_____

✍**EXERCISE 1-C.** Two words that you should handle with care are "thing" and "person." *Don't use them* unless you are fully convinced that either "thing" or "person" is the only word to use under the circumstances. The reason is that both words are about as general as you can get. Before using them, ask yourself if the "thing" or "person" could be specified.

In the sentences below, write an appropriate concrete noun over each underlined noun.

EXAMPLES:

                                                          virtue, gift
In family life, love is the most important <u>thing</u>.

                               teacher, mentor
Mrs. Jacobs was a demanding <u>person</u>.

1. That night, the wise shaman taught Angelina many <u>things</u>.

2. Most <u>people</u> don't like licorice.

3. Scott is the most exhilarating <u>person</u> I've ever known.

4. Their house is full of <u>things</u>.

5. Get this <u>thing</u> off my back!

6. Ross kept tripping over <u>things</u>.

7. <u>People</u> who need <u>people</u> are the luckiest <u>people</u> in the world.

✍**EXERCISE 1-D.** I hope you see what a difference a noun can make. Now try a short assignment. On a clean sheet of notebook paper, write a paragraph describing your living room. Your description should be **double-spaced**--that is, skip every other line. This will make it easier for you to add corrections later. If you have trouble remembering to double-space, mark an "X" at the left side on every other line of your notebook paper. That will remind you not to write on that line.

In your description, *be specific.* Chairs can be identified as recliners, rockers, armchairs, Queen-Anne chairs, wing-back chairs--if you don't know what they are, ask someone. Pictures can be paintings, prints, photographs, landscapes, still lifes, portraits. Floor coverings could be carpet, mats, braided rugs--you get the idea. Study the room, ask questions, identify, and write. Don't try to describe *everything* you see, but you should be able to fill one double-spaced page with no trouble.

✎ ✎ ✎ ✎ ✎ ✎ ✎ ✎ ✎ ✎

(When you see a row of pencils in this book, it means you are supposed to be writing. Don't proceed until you do.)

Proofreading is checking your work for mistakes, and it's not as easy as you might think. Once you've finished the description, turn to page 87 and read the section entitled "How to Proofread." Then read your paper carefully and correct any errors you find.

☞Here I'm going to teach you a new word and give you a warning at the same time. The word is **caveat** (CAH-vee-aht), and it comes directly from a Latin word meaning "beware." Just because I have been singing the praises of concrete nouns in this chapter doesn't mean you should never use any other kind. General nouns are necessary when you have to name a group including many objects of a similar type; they're also useful when you want to avoid repetition of a specific noun. All nouns are to be used. Knowing where and how to use them is one of the keys to good writing.

MORE PRACTICE. Find a painting in a magazine or art book that depicts a scene; preferably a scene with lots of detail. Imagine yourself in the picture and describe what you see, using as many concrete nouns as possible. For instance, if you're in a field of blue flowers, don't just say, "I'm in a field of blue flowers." You're standing in a field of larkspur, or columbine, or sky-blue lupine. If you don't happen to know these names, look up "Wildflowers" in a reference book and use the name of any blue flower you see--that's what those books are for.

JUST FOR FUN. Check out a field guide to trees from your local library, and use it to identify at least four different trees in your back yard or a nearby park. Some may be hard to identify just from the guide, but do your best. Then draw a map showing where each tree is and labeling it with its proper name.

2. VERB POWER

Nouns and **verbs** are the basic building blocks of any language. With nouns and verbs only, we could communicate with each other (although if we were that primitive, there wouldn't be much to say). All other parts of speech support nouns and verbs--explain about them; show their relationships to each other and to other nouns and verbs; modify, connect, describe, and nullify them.

You may remember learning about a class of verbs called **linking verbs**. The class is a small one: "is," "was," "were," "be," "am" and "are." We call these linking verbs because they "link" a noun with another word that describes or identifies it. Linking verbs are common. Underline all the linking verbs in this paragraph. You should find two, not counting the verbs in quotation marks.

Most verbs, however, show action, or tell what a noun *does*. Any verb to which the letters "-ing" can be joined is an **action verb**. Read down the list of words in Exercise 2-A below and mentally add "-ing" to each. Are they all action verbs? Even a verb like "sit," which isn't much of an action at all?

I believe one of the most positive steps a young writer can take is to cultivate a large "garden" of action verbs. That is, learn lots of them, and use the clearest, sharpest verbs you know to express what you have to say. Many action verbs bristle with life--they sparkle, snap, roar, race, buzz, pop and shine. But beginning writers tend to settle for the drab verbs, like "sit," "walk," "have." These serve an important function in our language, but they lack power and expression.

EXERCISE 2-A. Below is a list of several basic actions. How many different ways could you think of to do these things? Try to write at least three sharp, lively verbs for each action, as shown by the example.

You don't have to pull them all out of your own head. Verbs are so important that I've made a list of some outstanding examples and included it in this book. First, think of as many **synonyms** (words of similar meaning) as you can by yourself. Then, when your mind quits, turn to page 90 and check the list. Choose the verbs you like best or those that seem most expressive to you.

crawl _grovel, shimmy, creep, scramble, scoot_____

walk _____

talk _____

run _____

sit _____

march _____

say _____

shout _____

jump _____

Another useful tool for these exercises, and for all your future writing, is a **thesaurus**. This is not, as the name suggests, a small breed of dinosaur. A thesaurus is a book, much like a dictionary, which lists synonyms instead of definitions for each word. If you don't have one in your house, ask for one. Say, "Mom and Dad, forget about that mountain bike or CD I asked for last month. What I *really* want for my birthday is a thesaurus."

✍**EXERCISE 2-B.** Re-read the synonyms you wrote for "walk," "run" and "sit" in 2-A. In the following exercise, write sentences of your own using two of the synonyms you chose for each of those verbs. In each sentence, show what kind of person would walk, run or sit this particular way, and tell where he or she would do it.

    EXAMPLE: crawl

    (Type of person):   The <u>slave</u> groveled

    (Where he'd do it): before the king's throne.

    (Type of person):   The <u>little boy</u> shimmied

    (Where he'd do it): under the porch when his mother called.

(walk) _____

_____

_____

_____

(run) _____

_____

_____

_____

(sit) _____

_____

_____

_____

    Verbs can change the emotional impact of a sentence as quickly as the stroke of a pen. Compare these three sentences:

```
Jenna walked to the desk and picked up the vase.

Jenna stalked to the desk and grabbed the vase.

Jenna waltzed to the desk and hugged the vase.
```

    Nothing is wrong with the first sentence--it simply tells what Jenna did with no emotional "punch." But if the writer is describing an angry scene, the second sentence gets the emotion across without even telling us "Jenna was angry." The *verbs* tell us, all by themselves. In the last sentence the verbs alone tell us that Jenna is feeling ecstatic or triumphant.

    ✍**EXERCISE 2-C.** All the verbs in the following paragraph are straightforward and **neutral.** That is, they don't give us a clue how Sally feels--about Horace, about the stranger, or about the entire situation. Over the underlined words in the paragraph above, write verbs that suggest Sally is feeling very sad. You may refer to the verb list on p. 90 if you're stumped.

```
When the knock came, Sally walked to the door

and opened it.  She looked at the stranger for a few

seconds, then said, "You're too late.  Horace left

an hour ago."  Without another word, she closed the

door.
```

    Now, imagine that Sally has put one over on the stranger and is very pleased with herself. Fill in the blanks below with verbs that communicate her attitude.

```
When the knock came, Sally _____ to the

door and opened it. She _____ at the

stranger for a few seconds, then _____,
```

"You're too late. Horace left an hour ago." Without another word, she closed the door.

✍**EXERCISE 2-D.** Here are some more short paragraphs for you to rewrite. Decide for yourself how the main character is feeling (angry? joyful? excited? disappointed? sad?), then substitute verbs that express, or at least help to express, that emotion.

1. Ivan <u>ran</u> across the street to where the policeman was standing. "Did you see that van?" he <u>asked</u>. "It must have been doing 90 miles an hour."

2. Bernice <u>took</u> a book from the shelf. "My aunt wrote this," she <u>said</u>. Then she <u>walked</u> across the room and <u>placed</u> the book on Kendra's lap.

3. The captain <u>walked</u> to Sergeant Bates and <u>looked</u> at him for a few seconds. "Do you know you're in officers' quarters?" he <u>asked</u>.

☝ANOTHER CAVEAT: Words like "walked" or "said" are indispensable--the language can't do without them and neither can you. A close reading of any of your favorite books will show that the author uses lots of colorless, neutral verbs. The more verbs you can add to your vocabulary the better writer you will be, but at the same time, don't pepper your prose with so many explosive verbs it feels like a minefield. Experience will help you learn when and how to use those sparkling verbs you've added to your vocabulary. Keep cultivating your garden!

MORE PRACTICE: Think of your favorite board game. Write a paragraph explaining how to play the game, using as many strong action verbs as you can. Let your imagination run wild! For instance, instead of "Move your marker five spaces," write "Charge ahead five spaces and grind to a halt."

JUST FOR FUN. Think of a lively action verb for an ordinary activity, such as "sit" (straddle, perch, slouch) or "stand" (slump, pose, stoop, tense). Act out the verb you thought of and see if others can guess what it is.

3. A WORD ABOUT ADVERBS: MODERATION

Adverbs tell how, when, where, and how much. They can often be recognized by their "-ly" ending (as in "happily," "luckily," "suddenly"), but the adverb family also includes:

often, always, now (tell when);
very, just (tell how much);
outside, here, there (tell where).

Adverbs, like all parts of speech, are useful and at times necessary. But many beginning writers seem to fall in love with adverbs once they discover them. Be careful not to use too many adverbs, especially of the "-ly" type. Frankly and confidentially, too many adverbs can very needlessly slow down your writing and basically get on the reader's nerves. Truthfully now, can you see what I mean?

One goal of good writing is to say what you need to say without unnecessary words. If your writing seems too wordy, the culprits are often unnecessary adverbs and adjectives. The most positive step you can take in trimming the "fat" adverbs from your work is, once again, to add more verbs to your vocabulary. Many adverb-verb combinations can be better expressed with a single strong verb.

```
walked carefully -tiptoed, crept, stole

said happily -sang, laughed, chirped
```

✍EXERCISE 3. In each blank below, write a verb that says in one word what each of these combinations says in two. (Some of them may be hard. Turn to your thesaurus or verb list if you get stuck.)

said angrily _____   talked rapidly_____

walked quickly_____   said softly_____

stood sadly_____   pushed mightily_____

ran heavily_____   touched gently_____

spoke cruelly_____   wept loudly_____

I am not anti-adverb! Some of my best friends are adverbs. That's why I try not to overwork them; they tire easily.

4. THIS LOOKS LIKE A JOB FOR AN ADJECTIVE

Modify is a useful word to know when we talk about language. To **modify** means to explain something about--to describe, qualify or expand. The purpose of an adjective is to modify a noun.

You know how to use adjectives, but do you find yourself using the same ones over and over? The problem with adjectives is that the ones we use most often have lost their descriptive power. For instance, how many times a day do you hear the word "nice"? Could you write a description that explains exactly what "nice" means? Most of us probably say "nice" at least once a day; it's a habit. If "nice" were yanked out of the language we'd probably suffer from "nice" withdrawal. But I want you to make a little rule for yourself: "For the next twelve months, or as long as it takes me to work through this book, I will *never* write the word 'nice' on paper." Not even to write, "Thank you for the nice present you sent me for Christmas." The reason for this is not that I'm a "nice"-hater, but that almost every writer needs practice in finding adjectives that explain precisely what he or she means by "nice." Now that you've read the word "nice" so many times I hope you're sick of it, we'll move on to another problem adjective.

What's so bad about "good"? Vagueness, again. When you say the movie was "good," do you mean it was exciting? funny? suspenseful? spectacular? imaginative? With so many precise adjectives available, "good" should be avoided in writing unless you've thought about it and are convinced that it's the best word to use in the context. Notice how a better adjective can clarify the meaning of the word "good" in these examples:

```
good heart - merciful heart
good dog - loyal dog
good book - entertaining book
good man - honest and reliable man
```

Would you say that "merciful" and "honest" mean the same thing? Probably not, and yet I used them to substitute for the same word (in different situations). They explain what makes their subject "good." Usually, something is considered "good" when it meets our expectations, and we expect qualities in a book that we don't necessarily expect from a dog. In the same way, we call something "bad" when it fails to meet the standards we have in mind for it.

EXERCISE 4-A. How many adjectives could you substitute for the word "good"? Choose appropriate adjectives for the following nouns. You'll find a list of adjectives below the exercise, many of which may be used more than once. Try to think of some on your own.

_____presentation

_____song

_____king

_____costume

_____football game

_____student

_____teacher

_____book

Adjectives to choose from: thoughtful, noble, just, intricate, beautiful, glittering, interesting, exciting, clever, challenging, hilarious, melodious, moving, scary, obedient, intelligent, wise, and any others that come to mind.

If you were thinking of adjectives like "great," "wonderful," or "fantastic" to substitute for "good," consider this paragraph:

```
Our week at youth camp was fantastic.  Canoeing in
the river was fabulous and the pool was great.
Every night at the campfire an awesome speaker
presented a message that challenged us.  Our
counselors were wonderful, too.  The food was okay.
```

All that the underlined adjectives tell us is that the writer liked camp--a lot. But they tell us nothing *about* camp. The following paragraph conveys more information:

```
Our week at Sunset Youth Camp was fantastic.
Canoeing in the Hiawatha River was thrilling and the
pool was Olympic-sized.  Every night at the campfire
an inspiring speaker presented a message that
challenged us.  Our counselors were helpful and
understanding, too.  The food was okay.
```

No, I didn't change "fantastic" because that word sums up the whole camp experience. The rest of the paragraph helps us understand *why* camp was so fantastic.

✒**EXERCISE 4-B.** "Ugly," "delicious," "beautiful," "excellent" and "poor" are all respectable adjectives, but you can find better ones if you think carefully about the noun you wish to modify. The qualities that make a pizza "delicious" are not at all the same qualities that make ice cream "delicious."

Try to write at least two adjectives that explain *why* each of the following nouns are what they are. The first one is done for you as an example.

ugly   _____dress

_____building

spiteful, cruel, vulgar _____ remark

delicious _____ cantaloupe

_____ pizza

_____ ice cream

beautiful _____ garden

_____ hat

_____ sunset

_____ story

excellent _____ letter

_____ portrait

_____ cabinet work

poor _____ letter

_____ portrait

_____ cabinet work

✍**EXERCISE 4-C.** Adjectives also can also be used to express a wide range of emotions, as you will see in the following exercise. Think of as many synonyms as you can for the following words. If you haven't received your thesaurus yet, get a parent or friend to help.

Examples: angry - irritated, peeved, furious, enraged
           happy - ecstatic, blissful, content, pleased

sad - _____

mean - _____

lively - _____

fearful - _____

Take a minute to think about the adjectives you chose. Some of them may indicate **degrees** of the same thing. A young girl may feel *apprehensive* when she walks into a dark room, but *terrified* when she feels a cold hand on her arm. (And when it turns out to be her big brother playing a practical joke, she'll be *furious* at first, and *irritated* for years afterward.)

Also, you probably chose some adjectives that indicate a different *type* of the same thing. "Cruel" and "petty" are different qualities, or types, of meanness: someone who's *petty* holds little grudges and spiteful thoughts, but a *cruel* person takes pleasure in causing obvious pain.

✎**EXERCISE 4-D.** Put some of your adjectives to work now. From the list you made above, substitute an adjective for the underlined word in each of the following sentences, then write an additional sentence showing what a person who felt like this might say.

EXAMPLE A: The <u>happy</u> girl sighed.

The blissful girl sighed. "The situation couldn't have worked out better."
The contented girl sighed. "That was a wonderful dinner, Mrs. Alberti."

EXAMPLE B: Mr. Jones looked <u>angry</u>.

Mr. Jones looked irritated. "What do you want <u>now</u>. Roger?"
Mr. Jones looked furious. "Don't you ever come near my daughter again!"

1. The <u>mean</u> man laughed.

The _____ man laughed. "_____

_____ "

The _____ man laughed. "_____

_____ "

2. I'd never seen John look so <u>sad</u>.

I'd never seen John look so _____ . "_____

_____ "

I'd never seen John look so _____ . "_____

_____ "

3. The <u>lively</u> little girl squeaked.

The _____ little girl squeaked, "_____

_____ "

The _____ little girl squeaked, "_____

_____ "

4. Toby was plainly <u>fearful</u>.

Toby was plainly _____ .   "_____

_____ "

Toby was plainly _____ .   "_____

_____ "

☝TWO CAVEATS:

1. No rule tells you how many adjectives you can string together. But in general it's best to limit your adjectives, and remember that many nouns, especially concrete and specific nouns, can stand quite well on their own. Nouns and verbs are the meat and potatoes of language--adjectives are the salt. They are used to accent the flavor of your writing, not to overpower it. Too many adjectives can create a jungle, like this:

```
The witty, elegant and charming young gentleman
strolled across his spacious, emerald-green,
manicured lawn in the golden, mellow twilight.
```

2. Another pitfall for beginning writers is **colloquial** adjectives, those expressions we use in everyday speech and slang. Some examples are "weird", "gross," and "awesome," any of which have fairly narrow, specific meanings in the dictionary. But these words have come to have very broad meanings in ordinary conversation. Consider how many qualities the word "weird" is used to describe:

```
My brother is weird.
My brother is jumpy and excitable.

My sister is weird.
My sister is dreamy and absent-minded.
```

Because their meaning has been stretched out of shape, it's best to avoid colloquial adjectives in your writing unless you look them up first and use them in their proper dictionary context.

✍EXERCISE 4-E. To conclude your work on adjectives, write a restaurant review! If you enjoy eating, this could be fun. First, read the item on the next page or consult your local newspaper for a restaurant review. Notice how the reviewer uses adjectives to describe the food, atmosphere, and service. Underline or circle the adjectives, including the hyphenated adjectives, such as "deep-fried." You should find many that are precise and descriptive. In fact, you may be surprised at how many ways there are to describe food!

Center Field, at the corner of Lone Pine and Third Avenue, attempts to be both a sports bar and a mecca for "casual" dining, with mixed results. The menu offers a wide array of choices from deep-fried snacks to main-dish salads to burgers and fries. Nevertheless, inconsistent kitchen performance and spotty service make this more a sports bar than a restaurant. While some dishes were well-made and satisfying, others were disappointing.

The best of the appetizers were Center Field's big, crisp onion rings, thick circles in a non-greasy batter, served in a bountiful portion with a first-rate horseradish cream for dipping. Also quite good were Buffalo-style chicken wings, full-flavored and fiery. The spicy sauce makes them messy to eat, and while the menu promises extra napkins, we had to ask for them--and got one extra paper napkin apiece.

Less satisfying were the fried chicken tenderloins. The flat, dry breaded chicken slices came with a pile of mediocre French fries and two dipping sauces--an unpleasant honey mustard and a decent country gravy with bits of sausage. The chili comes topped with chopped onion and shredded Cheddar. It is deftly seasoned with plenty of beef and beans, but it suffers from a dull, pasty texture caused by too much flour.

Chicken cobb salad featured plenty of tender marinated chicken breast strips with a smoky grilled flavor. These were arranged on a bed of crisp vegetables and greens.

A 10-ounce Kansas City strip steak was grilled to order and fairly tender, but not spectacular. It came with an undercooked baked potato. Shrimp fettuccine featured thick noodles, slightly over-cooked, topped with lots of tiny shrimp in a bland cream sauce. Entrees include a basic tossed salad and crunchy garlic-cheese toast.

The décor at Center Field is strictly sports bar; the dominant decorating element is big screen TV. Still, it's not overly loud. Tables are spacious, and the interior is bright and clean. Service had its faults. On our first visit, we had to remind a harried server to bring items such as drink refills and a forgotten dessert. On the second trip, the meal was served at a frenzied pace. Salads came while we were still working on the appetizers, to be followed a few moments later by entrees. The table was overloaded, to say the least, not to mention food that quickly grew cold. When I complained to the server, she implied the problem was my fault!

Bottom line: Center Field works as a place for a light snack with the guys, but don't expect fine dining.

Now, ask your parents to take you out for lunch or dinner--after all, it's for *school!* If this is not possible, imagine you are "dining out" at your own house. Write a long, double-spaced paragraph, honestly evaluating the food, service, and atmosphere and using several specific, descriptive adjectives (don't use "good" more than once). Be sure to proofread and make corrections when you're done.

JUST FOR FUN. Look up the words "happy" and "sad" in your thesaurus. Choose three or four specific adjectives for each and draw happy or sad faces to illustrate that particular kind of emotion. Then ask a parent or friend to guess the adjective you drew.

5. WHAT *ARE* PREPOSITIONS, ANYWAY?

In spite of their long name, **prepositions** are little words we seldom notice because they don't call attention to themselves. Compared to all the other parts of speech we've studied, prepositions are few in number. In fact, I can list the most common prepositions in one small box:

> about, above, across, after, against, along, among, around, at, before, behind, below, beside, between, beyond, by, during, for, from, in, into, of, on, over, past, through, to, toward, under, unto, up, with

The job of a preposition is to turn a noun into a modifier. This concept is easier to show than it is to explain, and I'm afraid we'll have to get into a little grammar. First, circle the three nouns in this sentence:

```
The girl with the green hat perched on the gate.
```

"Girl" is the subject; "perched" is what she did. That's the sentence, stripped down to its bare essentials: "The girl perched." So what's the use of the other two nouns? "Hat" is found at the end of a little string of words headed by "with," a preposition. "With the green hat" is a **prepositional phrase** and it's used to describe the subject "girl." "With the green hat" modifies "girl," because the preposition has hooked up the noun "hat" and put it in service of another noun.

The other noun, "gate," is also at the end of a prepositional phrase, a shorter one this time. "On" is the preposition, and just like "with," it turns a noun into a modifier. But this time the word to be modified is not a noun. "On the gate" tells us *where* the girl sat. I hope you remember from Section 3 that telling *where* is the purpose of an adverb. The entire phrase "on the gate" is therefore to be treated as an adverb, because it modifies the verb. A diagram of the sentence would look something like this:

```
          The girl    |    perched
with the green | hat
                             on | the gate
```

Are you still with me?

The fun of prepositions for a creative writer is their "moveability." If you're not too old for cute word pictures, you can think of a prepositional phrase as a little word train, with the preposition itself as the engine. In many cases the engine can pull its train to other "stations" within the sentence. This is how it works:

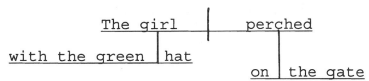

```
   In      many cases the engine can pull its train to

other "stations"    within     the sentence.
```

1. We could back #1 to a spot behind the subject:

> The engine, (1)in many cases, can pull its train to
> other "stations" (2)within the sentence.

2. Or drop #1 all the way back to the end:

> The engine can pull its train to other "stations"
> (2)within the sentence, (1)in many cases.

3. Or direct #1 and #2 to change places:

> (2)Within the sentence, the engine can pull its
> train to other "stations," (1)in many cases.

4. Or go completely wild:

> The engine, (2)within the sentence, (1)in many
> cases, can to other "stations" pull its train.

Obviously, some arrangements work better than others. Examples 2 and 3 are awkward, because "in many cases" modifies the verb (it tells when). Placing it so far from the verb breaks up the flow of the sentence. Also in example #3 the subject (engine) is obscured by a phrase that has little direct relation to it. The original sentence and the first rewrite work best.

✍**EXERCISE 5-A.** Prepositional phrases are fun to play with and could open up new sentence structures for you. Notice that all the sentences below are arranged with the subject at the beginning and the prepositional phrase at the end. Rewrite each sentence twice. First, move the underlined phrase to the beginning of the sentence. Next, move the phrase to a spot just behind the subject. Then mark the version that sounds better to you.

1. The soldier whistled softly <u>from the hedge</u>.

_____

_____

_____

_____

2. An unpleasant surprise lurked <u>behind the front door</u>.

_____

_____

_____

3. The crowd was having a party in <u>the smoking section</u>.

_____

_____

_____

_____

4. Kirby lost the race <u>in spite of his training</u>.

_____

_____

_____

_____

5. Sarah received her inspiration <u>under the walnut tree</u>.

_____

_____

_____

_____

✎**EXERCISE 5-B.** Write your own sentences for each of these prepositional phrases, then rewrite each sentence at least once, moving the prepositional phrase to another spot. Does it always work?

in the dark	above the clouds
within the mind	beside the bed
under the table	by the sea

✍ANOTHER CAVEAT. Sometimes a prepositional phrase adds little to a sentence except words. Watch out for the "wordies"! In good writing, *every word counts*. Some phrases to avoid are:

at this point in time ("now" is better)
for each and every one ("for all")
in the final analysis ("finally")

6. DID ANYBODY GET THE NAME OF THAT PRONOUN?

Pronouns act as "stand-ins" for nouns. Rather than, "Daryl swatted at the fly on Daryl's nose even though Daryl couldn't see the fly," pronouns allow us to say, "Daryl swatted at the fly on *his* nose even though *he* couldn't see *it.*" Thanks to the pronoun, we can add, "*It* was a stupid thing for him to do." **Personal pronouns** (such as "she," "you," "our," "him") and **impersonal pronouns** ("it") are easily understood. But the pronoun family also includes **relative pronouns, indefinite pronouns** and **interrogative pronouns**. We'll discuss relative pronouns in a moment. The others you may look up in any grammar book, if you're curious.

Personal pronouns can be a problem when two or more people are talking or acting at once. The writer has to be careful that the reader understands who "he" or "she" is. The identity of "her" in "Anne broke her necklace" is clear, but suppose that "When Anne and Mae went shopping, she broke her necklace." Whose necklace is it now?

Or consider this sentence: "My brother received a letter from the President when he was in second grade." Hold it! Who was in second grade, your brother or the President?

Every pronoun must have an **antecedent:** that is, a noun somewhere nearby which the reader understands to be the person, place or thing represented by the pronoun. In the sentence about Anne and Mae, the mystery of the necklace can be solved by making "Anne" the only subject, and moving "Mae" to a prepositional phrase. In the rewrite below, "Anne" and "she" are both subjects, so one is understood to be the antecedent of the other:

```
When Anne went shopping with Mae, she broke her necklace.
```

In the sentence about my brother and the President, all we have to do is move "when he was in the second grade" next to the antecedent:

```
My brother, when he was in the second grade,
received a letter from the President.

Or, When my brother was in the second grade, he
received a letter from the President.
```

If too many words go by without an antecedent, the reader loses track of who "he" or "she" is. This is especially confusing in a scene between people of the same gender.

```
The Cabin 16 pillow fight was a night to remember.
First, Katie swiped the counselor's pillow. "Hey!
Lights out!" she yelled. Monica swung her pillow in
the dark and hit her on the head by mistake. Soon
everybody was in on the action: Jeanne walloped
Monica. She got back at her with a smack that
knocked her down. Then she swung at Katie and broke
```

her lamp.

Before reading further, circle the pronouns in the paragraph above that are unclear to you. Did you circle all of them? It's anybody's guess who's doing what to whom with whose pillow. Most of the confusion is easy to clear up:

```
First, Katie swiped the counselor's pillow.  "Hey!"
yelled Pam, the counselor. "Lights out!"  Monica
swung her own pillow in the dark and hit
Pam on the head by mistake.
```

Giving the counselor a name enables us to identify her without hearing "counselor" repeated more than once. We insert the little word "own" between "her" and "pillow" to make it clear whose pillow hit Pam on the head.

```
Soon everybody was in on the action: Jeanne walloped
Monica, who got back at Jeanne with a smack that
knocked her down. Then Monica swung at Katie and
broke a lamp.
```

Here I combine two sentences and enlist the service of "who" as a **relative** pronoun--so called because it *relates* to a previous noun. In this sentence there should be no doubt that "who" relates to Monica, since "Monica" is the noun closest to it. Jeanne is then named again and the following "her" can be understood to refer to Jeanne, since both are objects. (If the writer wants to show that it was *Monica* who fell down, the whole sentence should be restructured.) Finally, I substituted "a lamp" for "her lamp" because by this time the reader doesn't care whose lamp it was.

✍EXERCISE 6. In the following paragraph, circle the pronouns whose antecedents are unclear. Then, above those words, use a proper noun, a substitute identification (such as "his brother"), or a relative pronoun (such as "who") to identify the antecedent.

```
Chester and Lester went shopping for their mother's

birthday present.  One of them wanted to look in the

jewelry department but the other preferred

kitchenware. He disagreed with the statement that

"Mom will think we're only interested in her

cooking." "What kind of jewelry could we get for ten

dollars and forty-seven cents?" he demanded. After

some argument he proposed a compromise, and they

bought their mother a basketball.
```

SUMMARY OF PART ONE

I hope you've learned something new about the old familiar parts of speech. To pull it together, here's what you should remember:

1. **Nouns are the naming words.** Use concrete, specific nouns whenever possible.

2. **Verbs are used to show action or to link a noun with another word that describes it**. Strong, vivid action verbs will add "zip" as well as emotional impact to your writing.

3. **Adverbs tell when, where, how, or how much.** Adverbs, especially "-ly" adverbs, should not be over-used.

4. **Adjectives modify nouns.** Adjectives should be specific and clear and not too numerous. Avoid colloquial adjectives as a rule, unless you are writing dialogue.

5. **Prepositions are used to turn nouns into modifiers.** The resulting prepositional phrase usually modifies a verb, but can modify a noun. Prepositional phrases can often be moved to add variety to your sentences, but the phrase should usually be placed near the word it modifies.

6. **Pronouns act as "stand-ins" for nouns.** When pronouns are used, the antecedents must always be understood.

7. **Words are the basic tools of writing.** Make every word count!

PART TWO: BUILDING STRONGER SENTENCES

A rich vocabulary is to the writer what fine fabrics are to a dressmaker, or pure gold and cut diamonds to a jeweler. The words are the material you have to work with. But words don't make language; sentences do. If you've ever studied a foreign language, you know that learning the words is only part of it--the easy part. You must also learn the **grammar** of the language, or how the words fit together to communicate thoughts, desires, commands, information, and ideas. Someone who knew only words, but not how to form them into sentences, could communicate only on the most basic level. He would know how to label things, but could them with he sense not make. Get it?

The finest material can be spoiled by sloppy craftsmanship. Imagine giving a bolt of velvet to a seamstress who knows only how to make potato sacks! The broadest vocabulary in the world will not help you if you don't know how to fashion it into effective sentences. Just like dressmaking, woodworking, goldsmithing, or any other craft, sentence structure is governed by "dos" and "don'ts." Like other crafts, these rules begin at a basic level and become more complex as our skills develop. I'm still learning some of those rules, after more than thirty years of writing. In the section to follow, you will not learn all the rules you will ever need to know about sentence structure. But by careful attention and practice you will learn some guiding principles--and perhaps even break some bad habits.

1. GETTING DOWN TO BASICS

Every sentence divides into two parts, **subject** and **predicate**. The subject is usually a noun or pronoun. The predicate must contain a verb. A sentence also must express a complete thought.

Unless you are able to find the subject and recognize the verb in a given sentence, you will become hopelessly lost in Part Two. We don't want this to happen, so let's review. The paragraph above contains four simple sentences. If you remember three facts you should have no trouble locating the subject of each. A subject: 1) is usually a noun or pronoun; 2) tells what the sentence is about; 3) comes at or near the beginning of the sentence. *Before reading any further,* underline the subject in each sentence of the first paragraph on this page.

Once the subjects are underlined, circle the verbs. This may not be so simple, unless you remember the two main classes of verbs, **action** and **linking**. Look back to page 8 to brush up on linking verbs, and remember that any word to which "-ing" may be added is an action verb. You should find that the sentences in the first paragraph contain both kinds of verbs. In the third and fourth sentences, however, you'll find another type of verb: a helping, or **auxiliary** verb. "Must" is used with "contain" and with "express" to give those verbs a sense of necessity (you might think of it as a bossy helper). "Might," "should," "will," and sometimes "have" and "had," fall into this category. Each of them gives a particular shade of meaning to the verb. Auxiliary verbs can be recognized by the fact that they always accompany action verbs.

The words in the first paragraph that you should have underlined are "sentence," "subject," "predicate," "sentence." These are all the subjects. The verbs are "divides," "is," "must contain," "must express." If you missed any of these, or had trouble locating them, STOP NOW, find a grammar book and review until you are comfortable with these concepts.

In that same first paragraph, I said that a sentence must express a complete thought. "Cheops built the Great Pyramid" (quick! what's the subject and verb?) is a complete thought. So is, "She sat." Both examples state a simple fact that can stand alone. But if I wrote, "*When* Cheops built the Great Pyramid," or, "*After* she sat," would these be complete? No; somehow we expect more from them. Now they look like thoughts that were begun, but not completed.

Incomplete sentences are known as **fragments**. Fragments are rather in fashion these days, especially in advertising copy. You've seen it. In magazines. To get your attention. Make you think. Sounds like someone is talking directly to you. But too much of it. Drives you crazy.

An experienced writer can get away with using sentence fragments *occasionally.* He or she knows the rules but also knows when it's okay to break them. Yes, writing rules can be broken, but only by writers who understand what they're doing.

This is important. A chemistry student doesn't walk into the lab on the first day of class and start mixing chemicals willy-nilly. He must learn the lab procedures, the periodic table of elements, and the chemical properties. Once he fully understands the basics, he has earned the right to experiment. In the same way, you must learn how to write strong, clear, complete sentences, and write *hundreds* of them. Only then will you be entitled to experiment with fragments.

For now, make it a point to allow *no* sentence fragments in your work. The one exception might be if you are writing a direct quote (more about that later).

2. SECRETS OF SUCCESSFUL SENTENCE CONSTRUCTION

An effective writer strives for variety. The quickest way to kill a reader's interest is to begin all your sentences the same way and make them roughly the same length. To see what I mean, read this description:

```
     (1) My room has pale blue walls and a yellow
carpet on the floor. (2) It has a bed in the north
corner. (3) I have a blue comforter on my bed. (4)
My room has lots of pictures on the walls. (5) There
is a dresser, and also a rocking chair and an
exercise bike. (6) I like my room.
```

✍**EXERCISE 2-A.** If the writer *really* likes her room she could try to make it sound more interesting. Look carefully at the sentences that make up the above paragraph and list each subject and verb in the spaces below. Remember that a pronoun (such as "it") can be a subject.

1. _____ 4. _____

2. _____ 5. _____

3. _____ 6. _____

What do you think is the main problem with this paragraph? Hint: Did you discover that "room" (or the stand-in pronoun "it") is the subject in three of the sentences? That "has" (or "have") is used *four times?* Four times is at least three times too many for such a weak verb. If you listed "there" as the subject of the fourth sentence, you were wrong, but it was an understandable mistake. The subject is actually "dresser," and "there" is an adverb (it tells *where,* remember?). "There" is also a wimpy sentence opener. The result of these flaws is a paragraph that could win prizes for descriptive writing at the National Boredom Festival. We'll shake up the sentences one at a time and startle some life into them, beginning with

```
My room has pale blue walls and a yellow carpet on the floor.
```

We'll make "walls" and "carpet" the subject, change the verb, and eliminate the useless phrase "on the floor." (Where else would a carpet be?)

```
Blue walls and a yellow carpet make my room bright and cheerful.
     or, Blue walls and a yellow carpet brighten my room.
```

The next two sentences could be combined and rearranged with some help from our friends, the preposition family:

```
In the north corner stands my bed, covered with a blue comforter.
```

Now we'll exchange a subject and verb again, and add details about the pictures:

```
Lots of pictures, mostly landscapes and horse posters,
   decorate the walls.
```

Next we'll do away with the word "there," discard "also" and shape up the list:

```
Other furnishings include a dresser, a rocking chair and
   an exercise bike.
or, A dresser, a rocking chair and an exercise bike fill
   the empty spaces.
```

Finally, "I like my room" could be rewritten to tell the reader why this room is likeable.

```
My room is a comfortable place to be.
or, In my room I can relax and just be myself.
```

✍EXERCISE 2-B. Compare the above paragraph to the description of your living room that you wrote back in Part One. No doubt your nouns are terrific, but how are the sentences? What would you change about the paragraph? Rewrite your living room description, including the same information but changing the sentence structures. Experiment; try changing the subject, or opening with a prepositional phrase.

Sentences are versatile, and part of the fun of writing is discovering new ways to rearrange them. One way to explore structure is through a technique called **transformation.** This usually involves rearranging the subject and changing or altering the verb.

Let's start with a pattern that should be all-too-familiar by now, the "they have" or "it has" trap which often snares beginners when they have to write descriptions. The verb "has" works better with people than with things. "Tim has a leather jacket" makes more sense than "The jacket has two zipper pockets." Technically, a jacket or room or town cannot *have* anything in the sense of possessing it. Here's a foolproof formula for escaping the trap:

$$\text{object} \longrightarrow \text{subject;} \qquad \text{"has"} \longrightarrow \boxed{V}$$

That is, turn the object (the noun on the right side of the verb) into the subject and substitute a stronger verb (SuperVerb) for "has."

EXAMPLES: The clock face has two golden hands.
Two golden hands adorn the clock face.

The house has four windows in front.
Four windows on the front of the house stare
unblinkingly at the street.

EXERCISE 2-C. Try transforming these "It has" sentences using the formula. In each example, the underlined words will become the subject of the new sentence.

1. My room has <u>a four-poster bed</u>.

_____

2. The cup has <u>a broken handle</u>.

_____

3. Our backyard has <u>a huge oak tree</u>.

_____

4. The Chihuahua has <u>an irritating bark</u>.

_____

5. Pride Park has <u>a huge swimming pool</u>.

_____

Starting a sentence with the word "There" is proper and correct, but beginning writers should never do it. This is because beginning writers often overdo it, and there is probably no weaker sentence construction in English than "There is." That's not to say that all your sentences have to be superheroes, but (once again) only after you learn to write strong sentences will you understand how to use the weaker ones. For the duration of this

WORDSMITH - PART TWO

course do *not* start a sentence with the words "There is." The easiest way to transform the "There is" construction is the same way you handled "It has": move the noun on the right side of the verb over to the left, thus transforming it into the subject. The linking verb "is" (or "are") can be retained, but with a little imagination you could do better.

```
                 There is a chicken on the road.

Transformation A: A chicken is on the road.
Transformation B: A spotted hen pecks her way down the road.
```

Transformation A is correct, but it doesn't tell us any more than the original sentence did. Transformation B is much better because it helps us see the chicken by showing us what she does (and adds detail with the concrete noun and the adjective).

✍**EXERCISE 2-D.** Using the formula again, transform these sentences to eliminate "There." Make the underlined words the subject, and try to substitute an action verb for "is," "are," or "was."

```
1. There is a fountain in the park.
```

_____

```
2. There are four children in the family.
```

_____

```
3. There was a hat with an ostrich plume on the shelf.
```

_____

```
4. There was a giant on the other side of the hill.
```

_____

```
5. There are three office buildings at Main and Strather.
```

_____

Another useful sentence construction is **active voice**. This is a point of grammar that's easier to show than to explain. **Voice** refers to the relationship between subject and verb. In **active voice** the subject is doing the action:

```
Active:     Cindy threw the ball.
```

In passive voice the subject is *receiving* the action:

```
Passive:    The ball was thrown by Cindy.
```

WORDSMITH - PART TWO

Notice how the subject changes from "Cindy" to "ball," but the meaning of the sentence remains the same. In this and the following examples, which of the two seems the more forceful statement?

A: Andy learned the new program in seven weeks.
P: The new program was learned by Andy in seven weeks.

A: Pop poked the putter into the pit.
P: The putter was poked into the pit by Pop.

If you said "active," you're right. Active voice is preferred for strong, vigorous writing. However, there are times when passive voice works better.

✍**EXERCISE 2-E.**   Transform these sentences--if active, change to passive; if passive, then to active. If you're confused about which is which, think about it: is the subject *doing* or *receiving* the action? You will notice that in sentences 1 and 7 you will have to supply a subject for the verb. In sentence 3, you may want to discard the subject.

After you've rewritten the sentences, mark the version that sounds better to you. But be careful! Don't just mark all the active sentences; sometimes the passive voice actually works better. After you've marked them, we'll find out why.

1. The symphony's performance was wildly applauded.

_____

2. Randy finally finished the race.

_____

3. They deliver the mail later on Saturdays.

_____

4. "The Gold Bug" was written by E. A. Poe.

_____

5. Many island natives were killed by the volcano.

_____

6. The question is being asked, "What can we do?"

_____

31

7. Our "little" faults are often swept under the rug.

_____

8. Men's souls are tried by these times.

_____

9. His own works praise a wise author.

_____

10. Susan loves all babies.

_____

Once you've marked the version of each sentence that you prefer, ask yourself this question: Which words in that sentence seem the most important? Circle the words. Do you see a pattern in the words you circled? I would guess that you circled the subject in most of the sentences. The subject is what or whom the sentence is *about*. It holds the sentence up, just as a fencepost supports a fence. Compare these three transformations from Exercise 2- E:

Active	**Passive**
1. The audience wildly applauded the symphony's performance.	The symphony's performance was wildly applauded.
2. They deliver the mail later on Saturdays.	The mail is delivered later on Saturdays.
3. His own works praise a wise author.	A wise author is praised by his own works.

All of these sentences read better in the passive voice because of their *subjects*. If we want to emphasize the excellence of the symphony, then "the symphony" should be the subject. "The mail" makes a much stronger subject than the pronoun "they." Since we want to make a point about a wise author, "a wise author" should be the subject, rather than "his own works."

Whether to use passive voice usually depends on which noun makes the better subject. For that reason, we're fortunate to have two voices to choose from. But don't forget the general rule: for strong, forceful writing, choose active.

✍ **EXERCISE 2-F.** Here's another room--a little out of the ordinary but described in a very ordinary way. Transform these drab sentences to give this room the class it deserves.

My room has four walls painted red and gold.
My bed is hung from the ceiling. The bed has a
Chinese silk spread in the same colors as the walls.
There is a trap door under the bed, which opens to a
heated pool in the basement. The south wall has a
refrigerator stocked with soda and ice cream and an
entertainment system with wide-screen TV. There are
big glass doors on the west wall, which open to the
balcony. I like my room.

_____

_____

_____

_____

_____

_____

_____

_____

_____

_____

_____

_____

_____

_____

_____

3. MAKING CONNECTIONS

Too many short sentences in a row can make you feel like you're tyring to drive in rush hour traffic: start, stop. Start, stop. Spare your reader this frustration by learning how to combine short sentences. Our language allows several way to do this. The simplest way to combine two sentences is by using a connector: a **coordinating conjunction**, a **subordinating conjunction**, or special punctuation.

      Coordinating conjunctions ("and," "but," "or," "for") connect words or phrases of the same kind: two nouns, two verbs, two prepositional phrases, two complete sentences. It's a fancy name for something you already understand:

```
Robbie plays keyboard.  Jimmy does the vocals.
Robbie plays keyboard, and Jimmy does the vocals.

A magician was next on the program.  We didn't enjoy
    his performance.
A magician was next on the program, but we didn't
    enjoy his performance.
```

      A **subordinating conjunction** ("as," "while," although," "since," etc.) makes one of the sentences unequal, and dependent on the other:

```
Robbie plays keyboard while Jimmy does the vocals.
Although a magician was next on the program, we
    didn't enjoy his performance.
```

I said "dependent" because adding the words "while" and "although" to the sentences above made them incomplete and unable to stand on their own. It may not seem fair, but that's grammar. Those little words look like prepositions but don't be deceived; their function is not the same at all.

      Certain punctuation marks serve as connectors; the best known is the semicolon look closely and you'll see one). Beginning writers, adults and children both, make the mistake of using commas as connectors. For example:

```
Robbie does the vocals, Jimmy plays the keyboard.
```

      WRONG! Those are two complete sentences, and commas cannot join complete sentences. That's a big job, and it takes heavy-duty punctuation. Use a semicolon:

```
Robbie does the vocals; Jimmy plays the keyboard.

A magician was next on the program; we didn't enjoy
    his performance.
```

      Semicolons were more popular in the past than they are now, as a glance at any page of a Dickens novel will show you. They are useful, but, like any other device, should be used in moderation.

Another way to connect sentences is with a dash--like this. Some English experts do not consider the dash to be a proper sentence connector, but the rules are probably changing. A dash can indicate a sudden break in the middle of a sentence--like a quick breath--before plunging on to the end. If used too much they leave the reader feeling breathless. Dashes can add a bit of dash to your writing, but once again--don't overdo it! If a page you've written looks like Morse code, you've probably overdone it.

4. COMBINATIONS

Simple connections are easy, but can become just as monotonous as short, choppy sentences. Fortunately, we are ready to move into a new realm of structure, where it's possible to take *part* of one sentence and set it right in the middle of another. There are several ways to do this.

METHOD NUMBER ONE. One way to combine two sentences is to remove one of the subjects, place the remaining predicate inside the related sentence, and set it off with commas. Example 1 shows how this is done:

```
A short sentence can be reduced to a single phrase.
This phrase can then be inserted into a related
     sentence.
```

```
A short sentence, reduced to a single phrase, can be
     inserted into a related sentence.
```

METHOD NUMBER TWO. **Relative pronouns** ("who," "which" and "that") are pronouns that relate a group of words to a noun. Relative pronouns can be invaluable when it comes to combining. Study this example:

```
You find the related clause. Then place it in the
     main sentence.
```

```
Place the related clause that you find in the main
     sentence.
```

A **clause** is a group of related words that contains a subject and a verb, but is *not* a complete sentence.   On page 34, we made a clause of "Jimmy" by adding the word "while." "Jimmy does the vocals" is a complete sentence--it has a subject and a verb and expresses a complete thought. "While Jimmy does the vocals" is *not* a complete sentence because it doesn't express a complete thought. But it still has a subject and verb, so it's called a clause. To help explain how clauses and relative pronouns work, allow me to use an illustration.

I am Doctor Cheaney, the famous sentence surgeon. On my operating table today are two sentences I will combine into one:

```
Terry limped over the finish line last.
He received the loudest cheer.
```

First, I will separate the subject, "Terry," from the first sentence and substitute the relative pronoun "who":

```
who

Terry        limped over the finish line last
```

The operation was a success in that it crippled the patient (that is, turned it into a clause--an incomplete sentence). This may seem like bad news for the patient, but actually it isn't, because I will next transplant the entire clause into the second sentence, using commas:

```
Terry,  who limped over the finish line last,  received

the loudest cheer.
```

The "surgery" allowed me to transplant one weak sentence into another, turning two weak sentences into one strong, flowing sentence. This is the purpose of combining.

METHOD NUMBER THREE. Have you ever heard of a **participle**? Did you ever figure out what a participle was? It's not that difficult; a participle is an "altered" verb.

A wedding dress may be altered into a party dress by cutting it shorter and dyeing it yellow. Likewise, a verb may be altered by adding the suffix "-ing." In both cases, there is a change in function: the wedding dress starts going to parties, and the verb begins acting like an adjective or adverb. How is this possible? Observe:

```
The duke stood up.  He accepted the challenge.
Standing, the duke accepted the challenge.
```

In this example, the "-ing" turns the verb "stood" into a modifier for the verb (telling how) and effortlessly eliminates the whole first sentence. Not bad, for one little three-letter suffix. Here's another example:

```
My cousin and I had a great time that afternoon. We
  played Double Dare on our skateboards.
My cousin and I had a great time that afternoon
  playing Double Dare on our skateboards.
```

Participles often collect words into **participial phrases**. To say more about the brave duke, we could show where he was:

```
Standing in the doorway, the duke accepted the
    challenge.
```

But be careful: participial phrases are modifiers, and their position in the sentence is important. What's wrong with these two sentences?

```
Eddie had a wonderful view of the Canadian Rockies
    riding in the observation car.

The maidens of Argon came out to meet the returning
    heroes singing their triumphant song.
```

Who were singing, the maidens or the men? Is Eddie or the Rockies getting a ride in the observation car? Because participles usually tell *how, where* or *when* the subject did something, they should be placed near the subject. Rewrite the two sentences above to make it clearer who is doing what.

_____

_____

_____

_____

✐**EXERCISE 4-A.** Now you know several ways to combine and connect sentences.

Connections:
Coordinating conjunctions
  ("and," "but," "or," "for," "because")
Relative clauses
  ("while," "when," "if," etc.)
Semi-colons and dashes

Combinations:
Relative clauses
  ("who," "which," "that")
Participles
Participial phrases

(If you are lost at this point, go back and review pp. 34-36.)

Rewrite each of the following sentences *twice,* first as a connection and then as a combination. In each case, mark the version you prefer. Use each of the above methods *at least twice* in the course of the entire exercise.

EXAMPLES:

```
(A)  Dotti sang beautifully.  She thrilled us all.
Dotti sang beautifully and thrilled us all. (connect.)
Singing beautifully, Dotti thrilled us all. (comb.)
```

37

(B) My uncle does leatherwork. He gave me this belt.
My uncle does leatherwork, so he gave me this belt.
  (connnect.)
My uncle, who does leatherwork, gave me this belt.
  (comb.)

1. Hester arrived late at choir practice. She apologized to the director.

_____

_____

_____

_____

2. Blaine stood up to speak next. He talked for twenty minutes on "Raising Night Crawlers."

_____

_____

_____

_____

3. Horses are beautiful animals. They are often celebrated in art and poetry.

_____

_____

_____

_____

4. Joyce Kilmer wrote a famous poem called "Trees." He died in World War I.

_____

_____

_____

_____

5. My mother was once a professional dancer. She danced the lead role in "Swan Lake."

6. Josh put a finger to his lips. He tiptoed across the room and out to the balcony.

7. The boy stood on the deck. We waved to signal him.

8. It started to rain. Sarah rushed outside to take the clothes off the line.

9. Water reflects a face. A man's heart reflects the man.

10. Mr. Hennessy showed us the cup. He said it once belonged to King George III.

_____

_____

_____

Although we've done a lot of connecting work, don't forget that not all sentences *should* be connected. Short sentences have a purpose. They are forceful. They get your attention. Longer sentences, on the other hand, create flow and rhythm for the writer's thoughts to move gracefully to a conclusion.

EXERCISE 4-B. Short and long sentences together make an agreeable blend, a lesson that some advertising writers should learn. Does the following sound familiar?

```
Comfort.  Serenity.  That's what you've worked for
all your life.  Now it's time to enjoy what you
deserve. Mammon Springs is your next stop.  A unique
retirement community nestled in the Florida
Everglades.  A relaxed, informal lifestyle to suit
your golden years.  Call us. We have a lot for you.
```

Underline each fragment in the above paragraph (and be careful--just because it's short doesn't mean it's a fragment). Then, decide which sentences or fragments you will combine, keeping in mind that the ones you judge to be most important should be kept short. Rewrite the paragraph, eliminating all fragments and restructuring sentences to read more smoothly.

EXERCISE 4-C. Here's the same challenge in reverse: the paragraph below contains only three sentences. How would you *shorten*, rather than lengthen them? Rewrite the paragraph so that it retains all the information but becomes much easier to read.

```
On the second day of our vacation it was really hot
and the air conditioner in our car wasn't working
too well, so we had rolled down the windows and let
ourselves be blasted by the wind all afternoon.
Right after lunch everybody started getting on each
other's nerves and Dad kept threatening to stop the
car and let us walk, until finally we passed the
Brownsville City Limits sign and started watching
for the first motel that didn't look too expensive
but had a pool. Within an hour we had checked into
the OK Korral Lodge, unpacked our suitcases, slipped
into our swimsuits, run outside and dived with a
```

glorious splash into the pool, which was spring-fed
and felt like ice!

✎ ✎ ✎ ✎ ✎ ✎ ✎ ✎ ✎ ✎

✍ **EXERCISE 4-D.** I could say much more about sentences, but it's time you started writing some of your own. As a "final exam" to the first two parts of *Wordsmith*, read the summaries on pages 24 and 42, then rewrite these paragraphs, incorporating the tips you've learned about words and sentence structure.

1. After the game we went out for pizza. The pizza
   restaurant was full of people, all talking and
   laughing. There were lots of arcade games. We
   ordered our pizza. Then we played some games. I was
   high score for that day on one game. They called our
   number. I went to get our pizza at the window. We
   ate the pizza, then played some more games. It was
   fun, except when one kid put his elbow in my eye.

2. It was a nice day. We saw flowers along the sidewalk
   as we walked along. Children were playing in the
   park while people sat and watched. There was a
   little girl riding her bike on the sidewalk. She was
   coming toward us. She didn't know how to ride very
   well. "Look out," Dad said, but it was too late.
   The bicycle ran into the person in front of us and
   knocked him down.

3. [Write another descriptive paragraph, this time
   telling what your "ideal room" would look like if you
   had permission to design one and all the money you
   needed. Shift your imagination to high gear and
   spare none of the lavish details!]

SUMMARY OF PART TWO

Let's review what you've learned about sentences:

1. Every sentence is divided into a subject and a predicate. The subject is usually a noun or pronoun, and the predicate contains either a linking verb, an action verb, or an action verb with an auxiliary.

2. Every sentence must express a complete thought. Fragments are not allowed in this course.

3. Sentences may be transformed by manipulating and/or changing the subject and the verb.

4. "There is" and "It has" are undesirable sentence openers for beginning writers.

5. In active voice the subject is doing the action. In passive voice the subject is receiving the action. Generally, active voice makes for stronger sentences.

6. Short, related sentences may be connected by a coordinating conjunction, a subordinating conjunction, or a semicolon.

7. In order to combine sentences it is necessary to change one of the sentences, either by removing the subject or predicate or by altering the verb to a participle.

8. Long sentences "flow" well, but short sentences are more forceful.

PART THREE - *NOW* WE'RE WRITING!

You have something to say. I don't care how many times you've sat at a desk with a pencil in your hand and a mind as blank as the paper in front of you--I still insist that you have something to say.

Do you think you never go anywhere or do anything interesting? What would you think of a woman who was born and grew up in the same house, never moved, never went on vacation, never had more than a few friends, never married, and died at age 56? It would be hard to imagine a more boring life. But Emily Dickinson wrote over a thousand poems during her "boring" life, which are still read and enjoyed (and required for every American literature student) today. Here's one:

> The sky is low, the clouds are mean;
> A traveling flake of snow
> Across a barn or thorn or rut
> Debates if it will go.
>
> A narrow wind complains all day
> How some one treated him.
> Nature, like us, is sometimes caught
> Without her diadem.

Poets often take the simple, ordinary experiences of their lives--like looking out the window on a dreary winter's day--and use sharp comparisons and vivid imagery to illustrate some aspect of what it means to be alive. You may never be a great poet, but you have *lots* of simple, ordinary experiences. Sometimes you even have extraordinary experiences that would have amazed Emily Dickinson. Your life is full of material, and you are the only one who can communicate it. Because you are one of a kind, you will experience your life in a unique way. Because you are *you,* and no one else, you will see and feel life a little differently from everyone else.

Some authors keep a journal in which to write their impressions of daily events--impressions which later find their way into novels and stories. You may be thinking, "That's great, but I don't have any intention of writing a novel or a story. I just want to get through this book, and I still don't know what to write about!"

Stop worrying--I'll tell you what to write about. You may even have so much fun you'll forget how worried you were.

1. EXPLORING SENSORY EXPERIENCE

You receive information the same way everyone else does--through the senses. What you *sense* (see, hear, smell, feel and taste) affects what you *think*. Can you ever hear sleigh bells without thinking of Christmas? The senses are like windows that open directly to experience, and people who live in the same culture share many of the same sensory impressions. Sparkling tinsel, the sharp scent of pine, warm gingerbread cookies, and smooth red ribbon are all images that say "Christmas" to many of us.

Try an experiment. On the lines below, write something about Christmas that relates to each of the five senses. Try to think of at least one descriptive adjective to go with each, like *smooth* red ribbon, or *sparkling* tinsel.

Christmas:

_____ (sight)

_____ (sound)

_____ (touch)

_____ (taste)

_____ (smell)

Merry Christmas!

Do you know what you've just done? You've written a poem!

Your poem doesn't rhyme, but poetry and rhyme aren't necessarily the same thing. In fact, the poetry you'll be writing in this section will almost certainly be better if it *doesn't* rhyme. The reason is that while you're busy thinking of words that rhyme ("Ummmm, 'plink,' 'pink,' 'sink,' 'stink'..."), you may overlook the very words that would best express your feelings. I have only one rule for poetry:

> Poetry is the result
> of choosing the words to say
> just what you want to say
> in just enough space.

More than any other kind of writing, poetry deals with feelings and impressions. This is where your senses come in.

✍EXERCISE 1-A. Think of your favorite season of the year: winter, spring, summer or fall. Each season has its own character, its own holidays, smells, sounds, activities. On a blank piece of notebook paper, write a poem about the season you like best. Don't let the assignment scare you--just use the model of your Christmas poem. That is, write the name of the season on the first line, write an impression from this season for each of the five senses, and end with the name again, modified by a descriptive adjective that sums up the whole season for you.

Do you like what you've done? Ask two people--a parent and a friend, for example--to read your poem and tell you if the words you chose suggest the season to them. You may want to change a line or two, or think harder about a particular taste or smell. When your poem is perfect (or as perfect as you can make it), copy or print it.

EXERCISE 1-B. Write similar poems about the other three seasons. Think about them, write your impressions, correct the lines, and copy them on good-quality paper. Bound together in a booklet, with illustrations, your original poetry would make a priceless, one-of-a-kind gift for somebody close to you (and it wouldn't cost much!).

EXERCISE 1-C. Now for a challenge. Try writing a poem about a color, describing how that color would taste, smell, sound and feel. Here's an example:

```
Purple looks rich, like a king's robe.
Purple feels soft and smooth as velvet.
Purple smells dark and sweet as violets.
Purple sounds like the mellow notes of a French horn.
Purple tastes dark and wild as blackberries.
```

If purple doesn't appeal to you, think of robin's-egg blue, or vermilion, or ochre. Think about two or three colors, and write poems comparing how they would taste or smell. Follow the pattern given above, or use your own pattern.

A collection of color poems would make an attractive little booklet, too. Maybe Emily Dickinson got started this way.

Poetry is such a huge subject I would have to write another book to do justice to it. I'll just say here that a poem can be about anything and take any form. The best way to become familiar with poetry is to read it.

EXERCISE 1-D. On pages 91-92 you'll find some poems written by young people ages 10-15. Read them carefully, and notice how *all* five senses are involved. Some of the poems have an obvious pattern; others don't. After reading these poems, write at least one more on any subject you choose. You might want to describe a favorite place, a holiday, a sports activity, a parade, a painting or picture, or *anything* that can be explored through all the senses. Make sure that you include at least one sensory image per line. Read your poem several times, and change words and images until it says what you want to say. Make corrections, then copy or print.

✐ ✐ ✐ ✐ ✐ ✐ ✐ ✐ ✐ ✐ ✐

2. FIGURES OF SPEECH

Look at the words "sensory image" in the paragraph at the top of this page. What's your idea of an "image"? An idol? A statue? A reflection in a mirror or pond? A **word image** is a single impression, a picture drawn in words. The poems you wrote contained a number of smells, sounds and textures that made impressions, like ghostly footprints, on a reader's mind. You recalled several concrete, specific sensory impressions to express your feelings about summer, Christmas, or whatever. These things were not in front of your eyes or within your grasp when you wrote about them. You *imagined,* then *expressed* them in words. They were **literal images**--word pictures of real things.

All written images are word pictures drawn on the mind to help the reader understand what the author means. Literal images do this by referring to sensory details. **Figurative images** accomplish the same purpose by comparing one thing to another. We call these "Figures of Speech."

Often the comparison is one the reader never thought of before, and the surprise of it will startle him or her into fresh insights. I've used several comparisons in this book. In the introduction, I suggested that painting a picture could be compared to writing a story. This was an extended figure of speech to help you see that the thought processes which precede both are much the same, even though the results are different.

The most obvious type of comparison is a **simile**, in which the comparison is signaled by the word "like" or "as."

> Jed is as stubborn as a rusty jar lid.
> Mary hums like wind through a screen when she's nervous.

On page 19, I compared prepositional phrases to little word trains. The preposition, you may recall, was *like* an engine that could pull its "cars" (words) around the sentence.

🖎**EXERCISE 2-A.** Some similes have become so common they are clichés (pronounced cli-SHAYS). "Ran like a rabbit," "flat as a pancake," "dead as a doornail" are so overused they have lost their power to startle. We no longer wonder what makes a doornail dead, or whether pancakes are all that flat. Fresh similes are hard to come by in conversation--few of us can think that fast--but a writer has time to capture the perfect comparison.

Many of the examples below are so overworked that a cliché will immediately jump to mind. Don't use it! See if you can think of something else that's heavy besides lead, or white instead of snow.

1. Light as _____

2. Quick as _____

3. Heavy as _____

4. Cold as _____

5. Slow as _____

6. Hot as _____

7. Flat as _____

8. Hard as _____

9. White as _____

10. Green as _____

Now try these:

1. Janice ran like _____.

2. Her eyes sparkled like _____.

3. Pearce grinned like _____.

4. The captain stood like _____.

5. Mrs. Blake screamed like _____.

Metaphors are sometimes harder to spot than similes because they don't make use of those telling little words, "like" or "as." In a metaphor, one thing is compared to another as if it actually *were* the other. On page 17, I referred to nouns and verbs as the "meat and potatoes" of language; this is an example of metaphor. Louis XIV of France said, "I *am* the state," not, "I am *like* the state." General Sherman said, "War is hell," and not, "War is really a lot like hell, you know?" From these examples, you may detect that a metaphor is often a more powerful statement than a simile.

Have you ever tried to describe an abstract concept, such as "justice," "misery," or "joy"? Metaphor lends itself well to this type of exercise. Notice how this fourteen-year-old used metaphors to define happiness:

Happiness is hearing that you got the job, after days
    of anxiety.
Happiness is holding a baby and seeing it smile at
    you.
Happiness is finally being able to open a container
    that you haven't been able to for weeks.
Happiness is being with one of your best friends.

✎ **EXERCISE 2-B**. Choose two of the following:

Joy	Excitement	Disappointment	Sorrow
Peace	Love	Satisfaction	Patriotism
Depression	Justice	Faith	

Define each of the two concepts you chose with at least four metaphors, as in the example about happiness.

Such expressions as "Eleanor's face clouded" and "Harvey flew past the judges' stand" are metaphors in shorthand. They make use of a verb to imply that the subject is doing something that's actually impossible. We know Harvey can't fly, but we accept the verb as a metaphor for his great speed.

Personification is a type of metaphor that compares an animal or object to a human being. Remember the word "person" in personification and you won't forget what that fifty-dollar word means. Look at the poem on p. 43 and notice how Emily Dickinson personifies the wind by picturing it as a petty whiner. What other personification can you spot in the poem? What is personified in poem #5 on p. 92?

✎ **EXERCISE 2-C**. A personification may be short and fleeting, or long and involved. Here are a couple of short ones. Notice how the verb almost single-handedly creates the image in each sentence:

A single elm tree stood sentinel in the back yard.
The tractor coughed tiredly, then died.

Think about the everyday objects listed below, then apply actions to them that are usually performed by humans. If you need ideas, the verb list on page 90 may help.

1. The telephone _____

2. The washing machine _____

_____

3. The daffodils _____

_____

     Now locate some objects around the house or neighborhood to personify. This is easier if you choose things that make noise or move in some way.

4. _____

_____

5. _____

_____

6. _____

_____

✍ **EXERCISE 2-D**. Another way to experiment with personification is to imagine that you are an inanimate object. Write a short poem entitled "I Am the Wind." In your poem tell what you do and how you feel, using verbs that are usually applied to human beings. If you like, you may use this format, or one of your own devising:

```
EXAMPLE:   I am the night.
           I prowl softly through the silent streets,
           Brushing against closed windows.
           No one sees my face because
           It's hidden in a dark, dark cloak.

I am the wind.
```

_____ (mention two specific actions you do)

_____

_____ (tell how you feel about it, and why)

_____

     Write at least two more personification poems, in any form you like, choosing as your subject a natural phenomenon, an inanimate or mechanical object, or an animal.

3. SPECIAL PLACES

When I was growing up, I used to look forward to going downtown with my sisters to see a movie. After a forty-minute bus trip, during which the green lawns of the suburbs gave way to concrete and skyscrapers, we stepped down into the diesel fumes and busy sidewalks of the city. Our destination was one of the four downtown movie theaters, where thirty-five cents paid my way into another world.

The theaters sported names like "The Palace" and "The Majestic." Although decorating schemes varied, all relied on mirrors and carved wood, gilded plaster, dark velvets, and wide curving staircases to create a luxurious atmosphere. But each lobby smelled like movie theaters everywhere--a heavy mixture of cigarette smoke and buttered popcorn.

My favorite place to sit was in the balcony. While waiting for the movie to start, I rocked my squeaky, velvet-upholstered chair back and forth. The domed ceiling of the Majestic rose so high I could make myself dizzy staring up into it. The soft crunch of the popcorn we nibbled while waiting has seemed ever since to be the very taste of anticipation. Finally the dim lights would darken, the projectors hum, the huge heavy curtains roll back from the screen with a whoosh, and the show began.

You know places that seem to rush at you with *feelings*. You walk into the dentist's office and the butterflies start up a flutter in your stomach, even if you've only come to meet your sister. The gym where you practice basketball makes you tingle with a mixture of anxiety and excitement. The oak tree in your back yard wraps you in peace and contentment every time you climb up in it. These places are loaded with associations, with pleasant or unpleasant memories. Every time you smell Novocain or hear the smack of a basketball on a hardwood floor, some of those associations come back.

✍EXERCISE 3-A. Read my description of the movie theater again. I retain emotional memories of places like the Majestic because I visited them for one purpose only: to see movies. They were places of anticipation, excitement, and escape from the everyday world. You may have noticed that the description is full of detail, and all of the details are sensory impressions. Write some of these details in the chart below. You should find at least one item to go in each column.

Sight	Sound	Smell	Touch	Taste

Our five senses are windows to the world of experience. Everything we know comes in through the senses and is processed through the brain. Your mind determines what you notice and what you remember and how you feel about it, but the information itself is the same for everyone. You know what popcorn tastes like. You may also understand the difference between home-popped popcorn and the slightly soft, over-salted, bright yellow variety sold in movie theaters. If you do, you've shared part of my childhood movie-going experience. By mentioning the popcorn, I've opened a window between my experience and yours, and that's where we meet. Because we connect over the popcorn, you can (I hope) read the rest of my description with interest because it has something to do with experiences familiar to you.

Suppose I had written this instead:

```
     When I was growing up during the early sixties,
going downtown to see a movie was a special Saturday
treat. The theaters were much larger and more ornate
than they are today. Even though television, still
fairly new at the time, was supposed to be a threat
to the motion picture industry, plenty of patrons
attended the old-time movie theaters. Thirty-five
cents was the price of admission for children under
twelve, unless the feature was a special engagement--
a "blockbuster" like Ben-Hur, for example. Then the
price might be as high as fifty or seventy-five
cents.
```

The above is a perfectly good paragraph, and if I were writing a report for school it might even get an " A." But it does not communicate any *feeling* of place to the reader. One reason it doesn't is because I took myself and my impressions out. For another, I included no sensory images--nothing to touch or smell. The paragraph may have interest for someone who enjoys reading about the sixties, about movies, or about low prices in the "old days," but it has no emotional appeal.

The communications company AT&T once used the advertising slogan, "Reach out and touch someone." That's your goal as a creative writer. It is through the senses that you reach out and touch your reader, even if your reader never met you personally.

Take a moment to look again at the Emily Dickinson poem on p. 43. We understand at once that she's describing a cold, gray winter day, but it may surprise you that she never uses the words "cold," "gray" or "winter" at all! Instead, the details she chooses to mention make us feel the "winterness" of her poem.

✎**EXERCISE 3-B**. Refer to examples #7 and #8 (p. 93) for two descriptions by students your age, then think of a place that has particular and specific associations for you. Often the place affects you most at certain times or seasons--your kitchen on baking days, City Park during a snowfall, a night game at the softball field. Think about the things you see there, the sounds you hear, the smells you smell, the textures you feel. List as many as you can think of (at least one per category) on the chart:

Place: _____

Time of day: _____

Season of the year: _____

Sights	Sounds	Smells	Textures	Tastes

"Taste" may be a hard one, unless you happen to be writing about a restaurant or kitchen. But keep in mind that you don't have to put anything in your mouth in order to taste it. Fear or nervousness can be "tasted" in a dry, prickly throat. Dust, rain or snow have distinctive tastes. Some smells are so powerful they almost register on your tongue. If you're a gum-chewer, the place that you're describing might be one where you typically chew gum. Think about it, and see if you can't put anything in that "taste" column before giving up.

📄**ASSIGNMENT 3-A**. Write a description of a special place, double-spaced, following these guidelines:

    a. Use some details from each of the five categories.
    b. Use specific nouns for naming things.

c. Tell where the place is, what time of day it is and, if outdoors, what time of year.
d. Avoid "it has" and "there is."
e. Tell what your feelings are when you are in this place.

If you were able to fill your chart with details, you don't have to use all of them. Select the ones that mean most to you and are consistent with these guidelines. Your description could easily run to two double-spaced pages--don't try to cut it short. And DON'T WORRY ABOUT SPELLING EVERYTHING CORRECTLY. Spelling is important, but not for the first draft. Stopping to look up a word could halt your flow of ideas.

When you finish the assignment, go back and proofread according to the checklist on page 87. Correct any spelling errors (look up the ones you're not sure of), then check to see that all the guidelines are included. Put your paper aside for a day or two. If at least 24 hours pass since you wrote your description, it will seem fresh to you when you read it again--perhaps you can even forget who wrote it.

Now we're ready to do some revision.

To proofread is to correct technical problems in your work--spelling, punctuation, etc. To **revise** is to improve the *content* of your material. At this stage you will determine how you might say better what you're trying to say. There's always room for improvement in a first draft. I've written plays, stories, magazine articles, and full-length novels, and I still don't expect to write a perfect copy the first time. As the author Robert Cormier said, "Revision is a writer's privilege--one that a brain surgeon doesn't have." Whether you think of it as a privilege or not, anybody who writes anything must learn to revise.

Chances are, you have access to a computer and know how to use a word-processing program. In my opinion, computers have not helped anyone to write better, but when it comes to revising they are worth gold for saving a writer all the tedium of copying and re-copying. My system is to write my first draft in longhand, make corrections and type it in a word-processing program, then make further revisions (on page 89 you'll find an example of how I drafted and corrected this paragraph by hand). Most writers type their first drafts--always remembering to double-space--and that's fine if it works for you. It may eliminate a few calluses on your fingers but won't eliminate the need to revise. Get used to it!

Now that that's settled, look at "Revision Checklist #1" on page 89. These are questions you should ask yourself about your work. Read the list first, then carefully read your description. Did you follow the guidelines? Could more be added, or anything taken away? Change anything that needs changing. Because you double-spaced (didn't you?), you will have plenty of room to write in corrections where they're needed.

When the description is as correct and complete as you can make it, copy it neatly or print it out. Then read it aloud once more, to yourself or to someone else. How does it sound now? If you think it could be a whole lot better but can't figure out how, don't be discouraged. If you keep writing, and keep trying, you will improve. That's a promise.

Now that you've completed your first real assignment in *Wordsmith*, let's recall how you did it. First, you **thought** about a place. Then you **organized** your thoughts by writing your impressions on the chart. Once you had some details to work with, you **wrote** the description, and the assignment was complete, right? WRONG! No writer writes it right the first time. I asked you to wait a day, then read your paper again and **evaluate** it against the revision checklist. You made corrections in the original draft, then **rewrote** it.

All these steps make up the Writing TOWER, a process which *every* writer goes through with every project:

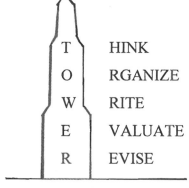

T	HINK
O	RGANIZE
W	RITE
E	VALUATE
R	EVISE

Writers who are serious about their work are "TOWERERERERs" because they evaluate and revise many, many times. Every "ASSIGNMENT" in this book is to be TOWERed. Are you ready? Here's another one.

ASSIGNMENT 3-B. Rewrite your description, but this time build some suspense and don't tell where you are until the last sentence. You may use all or most of the same details, but you will have to rearrange some thoughts and possibly use different words to make your place sound mysterious. The last sentence will be the "punchline," but by then you should have included enough clues that the reader will begin to get some idea where you are. Look at Example #9 on p. 93 to see how one 14-year-old did this.

ASSIGNMENT 3-C. Write at least one more full-page description. Make a chart and use the same guidelines as you did with Assignment 3-A, but this time do *not* use the words "I see," I hear," or "I feel". Think of other ways to express your sensory impressions, such as, "I shiver in the cool air," or "Laughter surrounds me." Remember some of your sentence restructuring techniques from Part Two. These suggestions may help you think of a good place to describe.

your grandparents' house

your back yard in the fall or spring

the roller skating rink

your piano teacher's house

the weight room at the "Y"

the center hall of a nursing home

the atrium at the mall

the swimming pool on a summer afternoon

Now let's go a step beyond. Do you have an imagination? Are you creative? Most grownups, when asked that question, will quickly say "No." Most young people might too, if they thought about it. We often associate "imagination" with being able to write fantasy stories, and creativity with making art objects out of milk jugs (or whatever). But everybody has an imagination, and everyone is creative, in some way or to some degree. If you can picture your grandmother's face, or recall the sound of rain, or replay in your mind the closing seconds of last Saturday's basketball game, that's imagination. If you can move these memories to another setting or use them in a story or poem, that's creativity.

Consider the following paragraph, from the first chapter of one of my novels:

Directly before me loomed the thick gray walls of the city and the towering arch of Newgate. A stony chill fell upon me as I passed through the gate, trailing its long finger down my back as I moved out of its shadow. Then I stepped into a broad swathe of sunlight and blinked with amazement, overcome for the moment. I had arrived: this color, this clamor, this dust, stink, and roar, was London.

The Playmaker (Knopf, 2000)

I have never been to London (though I would like to go someday). Neither have I time-traveled to the late sixteenth century, where this story is set; nor have I met William Shakespeare, as our hero soon will. But I have been jostled in crowds, smelled garbage and worse things, and know what the chill of stone walls feels like on an April day. So I moved those sensations to a different time and place, and used them to help get the story rolling. You may not want to exercise this kind of imagination for a few hundred pages, but you could do it for one paragraph.

JUST IMAGINE: Write a description of any place on this planet or off--so long as you've *never* been there. You may wish to use a picture in a magazine or book to help in describing what you see, but remember that you'll also have to tell what you hear, smell, and touch or taste *and* the emotions you experience. Make a sensory chart first, then write, using the guidelines for Assignment 3-A and your own imagination.

4. DESCRIBING A PERSON

When I asked you to write a description, I didn't ask you to limit what you wrote (beyond the mild suggestion that you might not want to record everything you see in a given place). But from now on you'll have to give some thought to what *not* to write. This may not seem like a problem to you, if it's all you can do to fill one double-spaced page. But one of the most important (and often most difficult) skills a writer must learn is to set limits.

Find a piece of lightweight cardboard roughly the size of this page and cut out the middle so that it resembles a picture frame. Now, in the schoolroom, bedroom, back yard or wherever you happen to be, hold the frame at arm's length and center it on one object or view. What does the frame do?

I'll tell you: the frame brings a picture into focus by blocking out everything around it. It helps you to concentrate on one object, one area.

TRY IT: Prop your frame up on the table or desk or windowsill so that you can see a specific area or object through it, while your hands remain free. Now write a short description (4-6 sentences) of what you can see through the frame. Describe colors, textures and sizes and make your nouns as specific as possible. Don't hesitate to use "action" verbs, such as "sit," "stand," "squat," "sprawl"--even if the object doesn't seem to be doing anything.

The previous exercise was supposed to help you concentrate on one object. Now we'll concentrate on one especially fascinating "object"--a human being.

ASSIGNMENT 4-A. If you are a human being, start with yourself. Use a small hand mirror, or move your operations temporarily to the bathroom. A mirror can serve as a frame to bring one person into focus. Spend a few minutes just looking at your reflection. Try to be as **objective** as possible--that is, pretend for a moment that the face you see is not yours. It may help to hold your cardboard picture frame up to the mirror.

Imagine that you are seeing this face for the first time. Judging from his or her expression, what kind of person do you think this is? Do you see a pleasant, friendly, thoughtful, anxious, serious, or self-conscious face? Write one or two adjectives that describe your overall impression. Now look carefully, and decide what it is about those features that give you such an impression. Alertness, for example, is often indicated by bright, wide-open eyes or raised eyebrows. Write down at least two specific features in your face that support your overall impression.

The following self-portrait was written by a fifteen-year-old:

```
     There stands a young man with his life yet
before him. His well-defined eyebrows over
questioning and playful eyes look out at the world
with hope and promise. His listening ears are ready
to hear. His strong jaw identifies a straightforward
personality, sincere and open.
```

Did you notice how describing the eyes and jaw in a particular way give us a clue to this young man's character?

Try it yourself: write a one-paragraph description of "The Boy or Girl In The Mirror."

Proofread to catch any misspelled words or punctuation errors, then put your paragraph aside for a day.

Read your paragraph again and return to the mirror. Did you write a good description? What would you change about it? Revise according to Revision Checklist #1 (p. 89), ask your teacher to proofread it, then copy or print it. Paste a photograph of yourself on the page and keep it with your other assignments.

ASSIGNMENT 4-B. Think about someone on TV who appears regularly "as himself" or "as herself"--a news reporter, a game show hostess, a used car salesman or furniture dealer. These people are not playing a part in a stage drama, but they *are* acting, to some extent. They are trying to communicate certain qualities that they want the viewing public to believe about them. The news anchor: serious and trustworthy. The sports reporter: upbeat and chatty. The game show host: witty and charming. The game show hostess: poised and glamorous. The used car salesman: mentally unbalanced.

Choose one such person on TV to describe in a paragraph. (If you don't happen to have a television, don't feel bad--neither do I. If possible, arrange to watch a program at a friend's house, or else choose someone in your life who acts in a public capacity, such as your choir director, your doctor, or your tennis instructor.) The challenge of this assignment is that you will limit your description to the *one or two qualities* of this person that seem clearest to you.

Now, observe carefully. First, what is the most striking impression you receive of this person? Second, what is it *about* the person that communicates that impression to you? What does he or she do with shoulders, mouth, hands, eyebrows or voice to create the character he or she seems to be?

In Section 3, you made a chart of sensory impressions to use while writing your description. This time I want you to make a **guidesheet** to help you organize your thoughts. This process will be the same for most of the following assignments. On a sheet of paper, write brief answers to each of the following questions:

a. What is the main quality you notice in this person (such as honesty, sincerity, friendliness, charm, wit)?
b. List at least two things the person *does* to give you that impression.
c. What details of the person's *appearance* (hairstyle, posture, facial expression) support your impression?
d. What does the person say (one direct quote)? How does he or she say it?
e. How do the person's clothes support your impression?
f. Where is this person? What's the most prominent feature of the background?

Here's an example of a guidesheet and the resulting description:

```
a. glamorous and glittering; "Isn't life beautiful?"
b. caresses car, responds to audience applause
c. dazzling smile, shiny pink nails, sleek hair
d. "A stunning new Chrysler Convertible!" she
   announces (promises? proclaims? exclaims?)
e. blue sequined gown, three-inch heels, diamond
   earrings
f. TV sound stage, new car, "Trust Your Luck" sign
   outlined in flashing lights

     Lawanna Dale poses in front of the flashing
lights of the "Trust Your Luck" sign and announces
the grand prize: "A stunning new Chrysler
Convertible!" The audience applauds wildly as
Lawanna's fingers, tipped with shiny pink nails,
slide along the satiny finish of the car. Her smile
is as dazzling as her blue sequined gown. On three-
inch heels, she saunters the length of the car and
pauses by the rear bumper, her right hand extended
and her mouth slightly open as if she were about to
say, "Isn't life beautiful?"
```

Notice that I didn't include all the details on the guidesheet, only the ones that seemed to contribute most to my view of this particular person.

Now make your own guidesheet, answering questions **a-f** above. Then write your paragraph, double-spaced; proofread for spelling and punctuation errors and put it aside for a day.

Reread your paragraph, make corrections according to Checklist # 1 on p. 89 and copy or print.

ASSIGNMENT 4-C. Rewrite the paragraph describing the same person, but in a different way. Beside letter "a" on your guidesheet, answer this question: "What *animal* does this person remind you of?" If he or she doesn't remind you of an animal at all, then look at him or her carefully and try to imagine a beaver, toad, bull dog, lynx, or other creature in the same place, doing the same things. Answer questions b-f in the light of this comparison. Our glamorous game show hostess, for instance, reminds me of a cheetah.

> Lawanna Dale poses in front of the flashing lights of the "Trust Your Luck" sign, her sleek tail twitching. "A stunning new Chrysler Convertible!" she purrs. The audience applauds wildly as Lawanna's shiny pink claws make a languid swipe at the car, leaving three-inch scratches on its satiny finish. She slinks along the car and pauses by the rear bumper, combing her long, elegant whiskers and smiling as if to say, "Isn't life beautiful?"

Remember to: THINK
ORGANIZE
WRITE
EVALUATE
REVISE

I asked you to describe someone on television because the TV screen acts as a frame to isolate one picture, even though the picture is always changing. The people you live with may be more difficult to describe because you know too much about them and could hardly write it all. I'm going to ask you, however, to write about someone in your own family by putting an imaginary "frame" around him or her at a given moment.

Compare these two descriptions, both written by ten-year-olds:

1. My dad is wearing a pair of blue jeans and a yellow shirt. My dad is six feet tall and very strong. He also has blond hair. He is slouching in his chair because he is very tired. But he is happy. He is sitting in a room with lots of plants and a big fish tank with a huge fish.

2. My mom was having a very bad day. She kept making strange faces, like her mouth wasn't working right. I asked a question and she yelled at me, "Quit talking and do your work!" Then my sister came in and started jabbering. My mom snapped at her, "Go upstairs right now!" My sister left immediately. I wanted to cry, but I know my mom didn't mean it.

The first paragraph tells too much in some ways and not enough in others. We get some idea of what the man looks like, and "slouching" is an effective verb to express his tiredness, but how can we see that he's happy? It's possible to be both tired and happy, but the writer should *show* the happiness by the facial expression or an action or direct quote from Dad. The writer remembered to describe the surroundings, but the fish doesn't contribute much to the picture--it's more a distraction. Better to concentrate on a few details that might show why Dad is happy to be home, such as the TV tuned to his favorite sports program or a magazine nearby that he's about to pick up and read.

The second paragraph concentrates on the person in a particular mood. Without saying that her mother was angry (until the end) the writer communicates anger by showing what Mom did and said. Because of a narrow focus, the second paragraph succeeds better than the first at sharp description.

ASSIGNMENT 4-D. Describe someone in your household. If possible, write the description (or at least make some notes) while you are in the same room with the person. However, he or she should not be aware what you're writing about. People who know that they are under observation become self-conscious--remember what it feels like when somebody sticks a camera in your face and says, "Just act natural."

On your guidesheet, answer questions **a-f** on p. 58. Pinpointing the most striking impression about your subject will probably be more difficult than it was when writing about a TV personality, because an individual who is not aware of being watched is usually not trying to make an impression. Two tips will make this assignment easier. First, describe this person when he or she is occupied in a specific activity, such as talking on the telephone, putting the baby to bed, or playing with the dog. Second, try to determine what mood your subject is in (cheerful? contented? irritated? anxious?) and focus on the mannerisms that convey that mood. Study the eyebrows, mouth, hands, shoulders. Remember how strong verbs and descriptive adjectives can help communicate emotion.

<u>T</u>hink, <u>O</u>rganize, <u>W</u>rite. Then proofread and put the description aside.

Read the description to yourself and **Evaluate** according to Revision Checklist # 1 (p. 89). Read the paper out loud to someone who knows the person you described. If you have a large household, it would be fun to ask your listener to guess who the person is. He or she may even have some suggestions to make ("But remember how Dad always whistles when he's happy?"). Don't be too proud to incorporate a good suggestion into your paper! **Revise** the description again, copy or print and add it to your completed assignments.

ASSIGNMENT 4-E. Following the TOWER steps, write a similar description of another person, either a family member or a close friend. See example # 10 on p. 93 for an unusual description of a friend.

JUST IMAGINE: If you could choose any sports figure, political leader, actor, or even fictional character to be your friend, who would it be? What would the two of you do together? Write a paragraph about spending time with this person, and show at least two specific character traits (such as kindness, patience, or a sense of humor) *by what he or she does and says.* Notice how the following example shows personality by action:

> My shot bounces off the rim, and LeVonne Bright catches the basketball with the tips of his long fingers. "Too much power, man," he says. "You gotta float the ball, like this." Dribbling down the driveway with the easy lope that makes sports writers call him "the Catman," he suddenly turns and balances on his toes as he sinks a perfect shot from fifteen feet away. "Don't sweat it." He has a big game with Detroit tonight, but he doesn't seem to be sweating anything. His white teeth flash like stars in a dark sky as he bounces the ball to me. "Loosen up your shoulders and try it again."

5. NARRATIVE WRITING I - SEQUENCE AND DETAIL

Do you know how to tell a story? Just put one event after another until the story is told, right? Wrong--story-telling is much more than a series of events, and sometimes even relating events isn't so easy.

Sequence is an ordered series, such as the steps in a dance or a game:

> Two people can play checkers. First each player chooses a color--either red or black. Then the checkers are arranged on opposite sides of the board, with all the pieces of each color lined up in three rows on the red squares only. The "red" player has the first turn. To start the game, he may move any checker on the row nearest the center to one of the red spaces nearest to it. . . .

TRY IT: To get an idea of how well you handle sequence, write a paragraph explaining how to make your favorite sandwich. You may dream up any delightful concoction you wish, but your sandwich must contain bread and at least three other ingredients that can usually be found in the kitchen. Your paragraph should describe the steps in order, leaving out nothing that's important to the recipe. Write it now.

Was that easy, or did you have to think about it? Did you have the sandwich together before you put on the mustard? Did the caviar end up on the outside? Did you cut the sandwich in neat quarters and stab each quarter with a toothpick, only to find that half the bread was missing? Read carefully through your paragraph again and make sure the steps are in order. If you were to give this recipe to your eight-year-old sister, could she follow your directions to make the sandwich?

One other thing: how many times did you use the word "then"? If more than once, it's probably too many. For variety's sake, consider other ways to convey a sense of sequential action, such as "Next," "After I spread the mayonnaise," "Once the pickle relish is on," etc.

ASSIGNMENT 5-A. Think of one of the chores you do around the house. Imagine that you're going to be gone for a few days and someone else will have to do this job for you, someone who's never done it before. Organize your thoughts by writing the steps in sequence, from the preparation (getting out any needed tools), to the procedure, and all the way through to cleaning up afterward. Write out a thorough and clear description of the job, and try to avoid using the word "then" more than once.

Now read your paragraph carefully and correct any errors. Did you name all objects with specific nouns? Did you use strong verbs to describe your actions? Could anyone complete this job by following your directions? Make a final copy. As an experiment, trade jobs with a family member to see how easily he or she can complete the task working *only* from your written directions.

JUST IMAGINE: Write directions for getting to a place in your city or town. The catch is, this place doesn't exist. You'll have to make it up, and imagine how to get there. Your directions may be based in part on real landmarks, but as you get closer to the imaginary place, the streets and landmarks will become imaginary also. Feel free to include tips and cautions, such as, "When you approach the River of Forgotten Dreams, be sure to start whistling 'Three Blind Mice,' or else you will find yourself remembering nightmares you forgot you had and it may hinder your progress."

When the directions are finished and copied in readable form, give them to a friend and ask him or her to draw a map from your directions. If that's possible, you've done a good job.

By now you should have a clear idea of sequence and its importance. But as I said earlier, sequence isn't everything. The following is a sequence:

```
1.      One evening last summer I went to the county
fair.  First I bought a candy apple and walked up
and down the Midway trying to decide what to ride.
I finally settled on the Ferris wheel, then I went
to ride the roller coaster.  That was so much fun I
went on the roller coaster again, and then I went
home.
```

But it isn't very interesting. Compare the paragraph you just read with this one:

```
2.      Dazzled by the noise and music and colored
lights, I crunched into the shiny jacket of my candy
apple as I strolled down the Midway of the Clark
County Fair.  "Hey, kid!" came a voice from the
arcade on my right.  "Try your luck in the duck
shoot. Three shots a quarter!"  I just shook my head
and wandered on, fingering the change in my pocket.
It was less than two dollars, enough for only three
rides--but which ones?  I walked the whole Midway
twice, changing my mind again and again as my
indecision became so sharp the candy apple almost
lost its sweetness.
```

What makes the second paragraph more interesting than the first? It contains some of the same information, but it also puts you, the reader, right on the Midway--offers you a candy apple, shows you the gaudy lights, lets you feel the loose change and the agony of indecision. Did you notice how all the senses were involved? From such details, could you connect this paragraph with your own experience at a carnival or amusement park?

ASSIGNMENT 5-B. Think of something that happened to you last week. It doesn't have to be anything special, just something you remember: a shopping trip, a bus ride, a conversation over breakfast. As you organize your thoughts, write answers to these questions:

a. Where were you, and what were you doing?
b. What was the sequence?
c. What did you hear? smell? touch? taste?
d. What did someone say? (If you don't remember the exact words, make them up.)

Write a short narrative of this event, one or two pages double-spaced. You don't have to include every detail on your guidesheet, but be sure to proofread and correct when you're done.

6. NARRATIVE WRITING II - FOCUS

An important element of every painting is **composition,** the way the artist arranges forms on canvas. Think back to *Washington Crossing the Delaware.* Without looking at the painting, can you remember what the main object of interest is? If you said "Washington," that shows how well the painter did his job. (If you did not, perhaps you should look at the picture again.)

It may seem obvious to you that Washington would be the center of a picture called *Washington Crossing The Delaware,* but keep in mind that the artist could have chosen to focus on the flag or right rear oarsman instead. The way he composed the picture--making Washington the tallest figure in the boat and placing him in the light just a little left of center--makes it impossible for you to miss the point. Part of an artist's job is to narrow the viewer's attention, to emphasize certain forms and play down (or omit) others. A writer can't use such visual aids as a frame, light, color, and perspective, but focusing the reader's attention is as important to writing as it is to painting.

Turn back to p. 63 and reread the two paragraphs about the county fair. We determined (didn't we?) that the second paragraph succeeded through the use of sensory detail. But the second paragraph, even though it was longer, did not cover the same wide territory as the first. We didn't even get to the first ride!

Think about that as you compare two more accounts:

```
1.    In January my mother, brother, and I went to
Snow Creek Ski Area on their "Learn to Ski for Free
Day."  I was a little nervous about going because I
didn't think I'd ever be a good skier.  We had to
wait in line for a while to get our lift tickets and
equipment, then we went out on the bunny slope.
    The first hour was terrible! I kept falling
down and it became harder and harder to get up and
keep going.  But one of the instructors stopped for
a moment and gave me a few pointers.  The day
improved from that time on, until I'd be finishing
one run only to head straight for the lift to try
another.  By the end of the day I felt like an
expert.

2.    The sun is lowering in the west as I grab the
rope tow at the bottom of the bunny slope.  I
squeeze my aching hands tighter around the rope as I
approach the steep part of the hill--my body's
tired, after a day spent learning to ski, but my
spirits are up.  I mentally mark the spot where I
plan to get off and--oh, great!  The guy in front of
me just fell.  This always happens. Somebody always
falls down on the rope tow just as I'm about to get
off, forcing me to change my plans.  (But sometimes
```

```
I'm the one who takes the spill!)  I make a hasty
exit and ski out to the middle of the slope.  I
glance down at Snow Creek Ski Area spread out below
me and the hundreds of skiers in colorful jackets.
I turn my skis downward, give a little push with the
poles, and suddenly I'm flying down the slope at an
incredible speed.  With my knees bent, my arms out
to the side, and my jacket flying out almost
straight behind me, I feel like I'm just barely
touching the ground.  This is the frightening part,
as there are so many unwary kids that I could run
into.  The shouting voices and the hum of the rope
tow machine all but disappear as the cold wind
against my face blots out everything else.  As I
approach the line of people waiting to get on the
rope tow, miraculously I slow down.  As I coast to a
stop, a man says, "Whoa, don't run into me!"  I grin
at him and say, "No way--I'm an expert!"
```

The first paragraph covers a whole day--it's a **summary** of the main events. The second focuses on just one downhill run during the last hour of the day. This is a **narrative**. A narrative is a detailed account of a single event. I won't insult your intelligence by asking which is more interesting to read. It may surprise you, though, that the second type of paragraph is also more fun to write.

Summaries are useful for condensing large chunks of information. In a story, they help a writer move quickly from one scene to another. But no reader ever got emotionally involved in a summary.

Think of the best vacation you ever had with your family. You could write a summary that gave an overall view of where you went and what you did, but without some specific details, I wouldn't have a clue how much fun it really was. On the other hand, if you tried to describe your whole vacation in detail you'd wear out both of us. The solution is to choose just one outstanding event of the vacation and describe *that* in detail. **Focus.** Remember the picture frame? The value of a frame is that it blocks out the surrounding view and lets you examine one area in detail. You must learn to do this in creative writing: "frame" one part of a larger whole to help your reader see it clearly. By "seeing" a small part, he or she will better understand the whole.

TRY IT. Let's analyze the second paragraph on skiing. First, notice how the writer manages to fill in the background in just a few words. Underline the sentences or phrases that tell us where she is, what time of day it is, what she's been doing.   The rest of the paragraph tells what the writer saw, heard, and felt during one downhill run.   Number the events that make up the action. Circle the sensory impressions.

⬜ **ASSIGNMENT 6-A**. Now it's your turn. Write two or three pages (double-spaced, of course) relating *one* incident or *one* special memory of the best vacation you ever had. First, think about it. Then organize your thoughts, answering these questions:

a. What is the *single incident* you plan to tell?
b. Write the events in sequence.
c. What background information does the reader need to know in order to understand what you're talking about?
d. What did you see? What did you hear? What did you taste, touch, or smell?
e. Write one direct quote you remember (if you don't remember the exact words, make them up).

Write your narrative, including many of the details you wrote on your guidesheet. Be sure to use some strong action verbs. Then proofread, make corrections, and set aside.

It's time to get serious about revision. Read "How to Revise" (p. 88), and think about the steps involved. Then read your narrative again. Does it express your memories accurately? Add any *relevant* details that come to you and cross out the words or phrases that don't seem to fit. Complete your revision according to Checklist #2 on page 89, and put it aside for one more day.

Read your narrative aloud to someone, preferably someone who shared the experience with you. Consider any suggestions your listener makes, and add anything to your paper that would enhance the story, as long as it is relevant to your focus. Finally, make corrections and copy or print. If you have a vacation snapshot, you may want to paste it on your paper as an illustration. Or, if you have a vacation picture album, make a copy of your narrative, cover it with clear contact paper and put it in the album along with the pictures.

ASSIGNMENT 6-B. Sequence, detail, focus. Now that you understand narrative writing, write at least one more narrative. Choose an incident, think about it, and organize your thoughts by writing answers to questions **a-e** above. You may use any of these ideas, or one of your own:

Write about an incident that happened during a soccer, softball or basketball game.
Write about a time you were embarrassed.
Write about a time you felt proud of yourself, a friend, or a relative.
Write about something that happened in church, on a shopping trip, or at the movies.
Write about a special moment you shared with a grandparent.

JUST IMAGINE. Dream up a moment that never happened, and write about it as if it did. If you have trouble making up a narrative from scratch, then think about something that did happen to you and consider what *might* have happened if the circumstances were different--if Joe hadn't listened to your warning or if your dad missed the plane or if that last-minute reprieve hadn't come. Use the same guidesheet for the imaginary narrative as you did for Assignments 6-A and 6-B and remember to focus on *one* incident. Also,

Remember to TOWER

7. WRITING DIALOGUE

Dialogue is what people say. It's the words printed in the balloons that come out of the mouths of comic strip characters. It's the conversation between actors in a play or a movie. If you've been following instructions so far in this book you've had some experience with direct quotes--the "exact words" spoken by a person. In my opinion, there's nothing like a direct quote to add interest to a story or description.

Direct quotes are the words of one speaker. In **dialogue,** at least two people are speaking and responding to each other. This can go on for a long time. In a play by Shakespeare, it can go on for four hours! When writing dialogue, a playwright or novelist has to keep several rules in mind. The dialogue must:

> advance the story or reveal something about the speaker.
> be true to the character--what that person would logically say.
> sound like actual speech, unless there is a good reason why it shouldn't.

That's a lot to think about, and it is not easy to do. Have you noticed that people don't *talk* the way they write? Suppose a Cub Scout came to your door selling candy bars to raise money for his pack. When you open the door, he says:

> "Hello. Cub Scouting offers a unique opportunity for boys ages seven to ten
> to get together, share learning experiences and practice skills that will help
> them develop into good citizens. Your support will help Pack 93 finance
> many worthwhile activities and projects throughout the coming year."

Would you suspect a "canned" speech or an alien from planet Talklikeabook? Those words, which look just fine on paper, would sound unnatural coming out of the mouth of a ten-year-old. You would more likely hear something like this:

"Uh, hi, I'm selling candy bars for my, uh, cub scout pack? Pack 93? You, uh, wanna buy one?"

Writing good dialogue means *listening* to what people say--all kinds of people, in all situations. Think back to an argument or disagreement you recently had with someone. The purpose is not to dredge up unpleasant memories, but to draw your attention to an actual conversation. Conflict is one of the easiest human transactions to recall and record on paper, but if you can clearly remember a conversation that was not an argument, you're welcome to think about that instead.

TRY IT: As well as you can remember, write down what was said by you and by the other person. Since you're not likely to remember the exact words, fill in with words that communicate the essence of the conversation--as long as they are words that this speaker is likely to say. Do not, just yet, write any **speech tags**, such as "he said" or "I replied." Record *only* the conversation, as if it were a play. Double-space as usual, and leave plenty of room in the margins to add revisions later.

EXAMPLE:
```
            "Haven't you finished your homework yet?"
            "I can't think today."
            "You still have a brain, don't you?  It's the
same brain you've always had, isn't it?  Why can't
you think?"
            "I don't know.  I just can't get started."
            "I don't understand how you can sit there for
two hours and stare at the ceiling while this
beautiful day is going to waste outside."
            "I can't help it. . . ."
```

* * * * * * * * *

Speech tags (such as "I said") are a little controversial. You may have read that it's best not to repeat the verb "said" over and over, but to use synonyms. I agree, but only to a point. "Said" can begin to sound repetitious, but synonyms such as "averred," "opined," and "stated," can sound pretentious, which is worse. "Averred" and "opined" are never used by anybody except writers who have been told to substitute synonyms for "said." Some successful authors use almost no speech tag except "said," but they use it so skillfully their readers hardly notice the repetition.

My own rule is to avoid speech tags altogether unless they are needed to show who is speaking or to demonstrate a change in mood. Here's what I mean:

```
            Mom stared at the kitchen floor and sighed.
"Who left these wet clothes here?"
            I stopped on my way to the door.  "Beats me."
```

Each character is shown in an action with the quote immediately following.

Adding "she said" and "I said" would be acceptable, but it's unnecessary--save the "said's" for when they are needed.

> "That's amazing," she said. "It's really
> amazing how little responsibility there is around
> here. In a family of grownups you'd think everybody
> might be responsible for their own clothes at
> least."
> "But Mom, I didn't do it. Honest."

Here the characters aren't doing anything but talking. However, since only two of them are present, it should be clear who the second speaker is. When another person comes on the scene, voices could easily get confused.

> Just then my brother Van came in from the
> garage. "Hi, all," he said.
> "Van," demanded Mom, "do you know anything
> about these wet clothes?"
> He glanced at me, his eyes twinkling. "Mark,
> why did you leave your soccer uniform right here in
> the floor where people can trip over it?"
> "Hey--" I began.
> "You're certainly old enough," he added
> solemnly, "to be responsible for your own clothes."
> "You know perfectly well--"
> "All right, you two," Mom said. "You both know
> where the laundry room is. In five minutes I want
> to see these clothes picked up."

Read over the entire dialogue again and, to the left of each line, indicate who's speaking--Mom, Van, or Mark. Which lines did not use speech tags? Were you ever confused about who was speaking? If so, what would you change?

TRY IT AGAIN: Go back to the dialogue you wrote earlier and think of at least two actions that show what the speaker is doing as he or she talks. (You probably noticed that these actions can also help reveal the mood of the speaker: "Mom sighed," "He glanced at me, his eyes twinkling.") Write in the actions, add any necessary speech tags, read the dialogue again and *listen* to it. Does it sound real? Share it, if you dare, with the other participant in this conversation.

EXAMPLE:
> Mom paused in the doorway, her arms full of grocery
> bags. "Haven't you finished your homework <u>yet</u>?"
> "I can't think today," I muttered, chipping
> paint from the pencil with my thumbnail.
> "You still have a brain, don't you? It's the
> same brain you've always had, isn't it? Why can't
> you think?"
> "I don't know. I just can't get started." I

```
scratched my ankle, resentfully.  Always the same
lecture.  She just didn't know what it was like to
feel stupid.
          She tapped her foot.  "I don't understand how
you can sit there for two hours . . . ."
```

Interviews are another way of capturing speech. They take a one-sided approach in that one speaker is asking all the questions while another is giving all the answers. This differs from the give-and-take of true dialogue, but it's a good way to practice writing direct quotes.

ASSIGNMENT 7-A. Choose someone to interview about a specific topic. If you think you don't know anybody interesting, think again:

> Ask a grandparent about his or her reactions to the Japanese bombing of Pearl Harbor.
> Ask your scout leaders what they consider to be the greatest problems facing youth today.
> Ask your parents how schools, shopping malls, or entertainment have changed since they were kids.
> Ask your state representative his or her views on education, government spending, or any issue that you're concerned about.
> Ask your doctor what he or she believes to be the most serious health problem in America.
> Ask your music teacher how he or she became interested in music.

If none of these appeal to you, look around at the people you know. You may be surprised how many have done something unusual at least once in their lives. Arrange an interview with your chosen subject, then follow these steps:

1. Before the interview, write a list of three to five questions to ask--a good interviewer always does some background work and has an idea of the area he or she wants to cover.

2. Find a comfortable place to conduct the interview, and as your subject answers your questions, write down a short version of what he or she says. That is, only the most important phrases--obviously you can't write fast enough to get it all down. To make it easier on yourself, take a portable tape recorder along, but be sure to ask your subject if it's okay to record the conversation.

3. As your subject answers, try to listen for speech patterns. Few of us talk like a written page, and everybody has a unique way of expressing himself orally. Some say "you know" at least five times a minute, others employ "really" as an intensifier for every other adjective. Some have a habit of *emphasizing* every other *word* they *say.* Later, when you write the interview, you will not be able to reproduce your subject's answers word for word, but try to include some of those patterns.

4. As soon as possible, write a draft copy of the interview. Pretend you do not know the

subject personally, and write as though you were meeting him or her for the first time. On your guidesheet, answer these questions:

a. Who is this person? What are the accomplishments or experiences that entitle him or her to talk about the topic at hand?
b. What is the setting for the interview? What can you hear or smell? If you are in the subject's own home, what details of the area reflect the subject's personality or interests?
c. What aspects of this person (voice, appearance, facial expression, etc.) make the strongest impression on you?
d. What actions indicate how the subject feels about the topic?

Questions **a-c** should be answered in an introductory paragraph. Question **d** should be incorporated in the interview. Study how the questions are answered in the following example, then write your first draft of the interview.

EXAMPLE:

Eve Simon, also known to certain people as "Grandma," was waiting for me in her comfortable, slightly cluttered sunroom. She is an attractive lady with a warm, welcoming smile and gray streaks in her dark hair. Stacks of books and magazines around the room showed her love of reading. Mrs. Simon recently celebrated her seventieth birthday but her memory is clear and her life has been very full.

"Mrs. Simon," I began, "what is the most vivid memory you have of the Depression?"

She looked down at the wrinkled hands in her lap, her eyebrows drawn together in thought. "A black Easter dress."

"Er ...How's that?"

"A black Easter dress. My mother always made me a dress for Easter, you see, but one year all we had was black goods. That was all. So she made me a dress out of black." Mrs. Simon shook her head with regret. "I knew she had done her best but I was _so_ ashamed of that dress. . . ."

After you've written your interview, proofread for spelling and grammatical errors, then put aside.

Reread your interview and make any changes suggested by Revision Checklist #2. Ask someone who knows your subject to read the interview and judge whether you represented that person accurately. If so, copy or print and consider including it in a family newsletter or sending it to a school publication.

JUST IMAGINE: If you could talk to anyone in history, fiction, or today's news, who would it be? What would you ask him or her? Following the steps above, imagine conducting an interview with this person. Write about the experience in two or three double-spaced pages.

TOWER Power!

The very best practice for writing dialogue is the radio play. A stage or screenplay writer can use action as well as dialogue to tell the story, but a radio playwright has *only* dialogue to work with--plus a little support from sound effects. The following example shows how a short narrative can be communicated through dialogue:

```
NARRATIVE: The second time Sophie came home late, Aunt
    Matilda was waiting up.  There followed a memorable
    row.

DIALOGUE:
(Squeaking door)
AUNT MATILDA: Do you know what time it is, young woman?
SOPHIE: Oh!  Aunt, you startled me.
AM: This is the second night in a week you've crept home
    past 10:00.  I expect an explanation.
S: Please, Aunt. I'm so tired.  Can we talk about this
    in the morning?
AM: No, indeed.  I demand to know what you're doing out
    so late.
S: I. . .I'm afraid I can't tell you.
AM: Can't tell me?  Such impudence!  Is this the way my
    generosity is rewarded? All the months I've fed and
    sheltered you . . .
```

Notice how much the dialogue can tell us about the characters. We gather that Sophie, though young, is old enough to be out alone after dark, that she has a secret of some kind, and that she is living with her aunt. We can also guess that the Aunt is a difficult person to live with. (Further developments, however, may prove that Aunt Matilda is justified in her suspicions and may even turn out to be the hero of the story.)

ASSIGNMENT 7-B. To try your hand at a radio play, choose one of the following narratives to tell in dialogue form. (If you prefer, you may choose another passage from a book or magazine, fiction or non-fiction--but your choice should be pure narrative, with no dialogue.) Determine the characters involved, name them if necessary, and write a short episode in the play. You must communicate all the action in the narrative using *dialogue* *only.* You may add sound effects where they apply.

Sir Lancelot approached the castle of the Black Knight and saw the ten shields of the captured knights hanging on trees, just as the lady had told him. He rode up and pounded upon the nearest shield. Just a few moments later the Black Knight himself galloped into view, fully armed upon a huge battle charger and fearsome to behold, with another captured knight thrown across his saddle. The villain demanded to know Lancelot's business. Good Sir Lancelot explained, courteously enough, that he was here to rescue the captives and would be pleased at all events to do it peaceably.

I am sorry to say that Peter was not very well during the evening. His mother put him to bed, and made some camomile tea; and she gave a dose of it to Peter!
"One table-spoonful to be taken at bedtime."
But Flopsy, Mopsy and Cottontail had bread and milk and blackberries for supper.

Beatrix Potter, The Tale of Peter Rabbit

Up and down the former battle lines, rumors buzzed. The men found it hard to believe that the event they had waited and prayed for so long might actually be at hand. Obviously a truce had been called--the very silence felt eerie. Soon word passed down the line that General Grant and General Lee were going to meet in the little village that lay between the two lines: Appomattox. Could it be that Lee was going to surrender? Could it be, on this quiet Palm Sunday, that the guns would stop, and they would all live to see Easter? And might they live to tell their children and grandchildren about the long and bloody war that ended with the United States still united?

* * * * * * * * * *

As you may have discovered, a disadvantage of dialogue is that it takes up much more space than narrative. Too much dialogue can also drag down the action. But when used well, dialogue is pure gold for making characters come alive, revealing their motives, and giving the reader a sense of "being there."

8. POINT OF VIEW

Your point of view is the way you see the world. Your interpretation of that disagreement you had with your little brother last Saturday will be different from your little brother's, because he remembers it from his point of view and you remember it from yours. His point of view may not make any sense to you, because it's bound up in who he is and how *he* sees the world. We experience different lives; we possess different talents. Your special gifts, your experiences, your attitudes and values all contribute to your point of view.

But one of the advantages of creative writing is that you don't have to stick to your own point of view. A writer learns to use his or her imagination to experiment, to step into someone else's place for a while, to look at a situation from another angle. This is not only instructive--it can be fun!

TRY IT: To practice expanding your point of view, start with something close at hand--literally. If your pencil could experience its surroundings as you do, what do you suppose it would feel? Pick up your pencil now, and on the top line of a clean sheet of notebook paper write, "I Am a Pencil." Put yourself in your pencil's place and imagine how it might feel right now while you're using it to write a paragraph. Do you suppose it leads an exciting life, or thinks it does? Pretend it can tell all, and write a paragraph explaining what it feels. When you're done, reread the paragraph and make any corrections or additions that need to be made. Read your paragraph to a friend or parent. Can he or she sympathize with your pencil's feelings?

I remember a popular song of the late sixties called "Walk a Mile in My Shoes." If you can "walk" so much as a paragraph in someone else's shoes, you're on your way to understanding point of view--and, as a benefit, you may be much closer to understanding other people.

This is a good place to discuss the three "persons." Referring to oneself as "I" in any form of writing is called **First Person**:

`I'm determined to do my best at creative writing.`

Writing in first person comes naturally to most people, and since I've asked you to write about your own experiences many times in this book, you have had plenty of practice at it. **Second Person** ("you") occupies an insecure place in formal writing. Sometimes second person is used in instructional literature, such as this book:

`You should determine to do your best at creative writing.`

The second person is "understood" in any command or direction. In a sentence like "Put the water on the stove," for example, the subject is missing, but is assumed to be "you." The use of second person is limited. I've seen editorials, stories, sometimes even entire novels written in second person, but that doesn't mean it's always a good idea.

Whoever is not "you" or "I" is the **Third Person**: "he," "she," "we," "they," or possibly "it."

```
She is determined to do her best at creative writing.
```

TRY IT AGAIN: Take that conversation you wrote in Section 7--the argument, if that's what it was. Stretch your imagination and take the other person's side (if this was a serious argument, you may have to stretch your imagination a *lot*). How do you suppose your sister was feeling when she accused you of reading her diary--even if she was wrong? What would be going through your Dad's mind after he noticed you missed taking out the trash again? Think about it, then rewrite that conversation from the other person's point of view. Write as if *you* were that person. Include a sentence or two showing how the situation developed.

EXAMPLE: Here's how the conversation on page 69 might seem from Mom's point of view:

```
      I paused in Kirby's doorway, my arms full of
groceries.  He was still sitting at his desk,
tapping his blank paper with a pencil.  That's
exactly where he was when I left for Food Barn!
"Haven't you finished your homework yet?"  I
exclaimed.
      "I can't think today."
      "You still have a brain, don't you?  It's the
same brain you've always had, isn't it?  Why can't
you think?"
      "I don't know," he whined.  "I just can't get
started."
      I sighed, completely at a loss how to motivate
him.  How could a bright boy be so lazy?  "I don't
understand how you can sit there for two hours. . ."
```

📄 **ASSIGNMENT 8**. Go back to the section on narrative and choose any of the narratives you wrote--about your vacation, for example. If you are a step ahead of me you will already have guessed that next you'll be rewriting the narrative from another point of view. That's exactly what you'll do, but you have three choices:

1. Rewrite the narrative from the point of view of another person in the story.
2. Rewrite the narrative from the point of view of an animal or an object in the story.
3. Rewrite the narrative entirely in third person--instead of "*I* did twelve push-ups,"
   for example, you would write, "*he* [or your name] did twelve push-ups." If you

follow this option, try to give some indication of how all the characters are feeling. This is called the "author omniscient" point of view because it assumes that the author knows everything (or thinks he does).

Think about how your chosen character (or characters, if you're writing in third person) would perceive the incident, then organize your thoughts on a guidesheet, answering the questions for narrative on p. 66. Write a narrative of at least three double-spaced pages. Don't forget to proofread, and set it aside for a day.

✎ ✎ ✎ ✎ ✎ ✎ ✎ ✎ ✎ ✎ ✎

Read the narrative again and ask yourself if you represented the feelings of your character(s) fairly. Then revise according to Revision Checklist #2, copy or print and keep it with your original narrative.

JUST IMAGINE: Think about a scene in your favorite movie or a book. The scene should include at least two characters. Write a short version (two or three paragraphs) of that scene in which you take the part of one of the characters. Write in first person, imagining the character's feelings, describing the situation from his or her point of view and including any dialogue you can remember.

✎ ✎ ✎ ✎ ✎ ✎ ✎ ✎ ✎ ✎ ✎

Write the same scene again, but from another character's point of view. This person will understand (or not understand) the situation from a different angle, a different set of values, possibly even a different location. Your two versions should make those differences apparent to the reader. Write the second version, then put them both aside.

✎ ✎ ✎ ✎ ✎ ✎ ✎ ✎ ✎ ✎ ✎

Reread both versions of the scene and add any details you think would improve them. Revise according to Revision Checklist #2, then write or print your final copy.

If you've written a scene out of a book, the author of the book would probably be interested in reading it. Most authors (assuming they're still alive), are delighted to hear from their readers, and may even take the time to reply. Authors may be reached by addressing mail to them in care of the publisher, and your library can supply the address of any publishing house. Or you may be able to reach the author through his or her website.

9. STORY

A. What is a story?

You may think you've already written stories in this course, but think again. Narratives, strictly speaking, are not stories. The two may seem just alike, but they differ in purpose.

The purpose of a narrative is simply to tell (in a vivid and entertaining manner, of course) what happened. That's why we spent some time in sequencing and detail. The purpose of a story goes beyond telling what happened. The story writer may wish to show *why* it happened, or explain the effect of the action on the characters involved.

A story writer will give more attention to some scenes than others, will dwell on some details and pass over others, may even rearrange events in order to make a point or create a mood. "Focusing" (remember?) is a vital part of story writing. So is good sentence structure, sound description, concrete nouns, strong verbs, and everything else we have studied in this book. When writing a story, a writer uses all of his of her skills to say something--to make a point or communicate a message.

Several years ago, when I was on vacation in the northwest, my purse was stolen. All my cash, credit cards and checks were suddenly gone. I did have a suitcase and a car with half a tank of gas, but no money for food or lodging. A narrative about that vacation would have told what happened (preferably just one part of it in detail) but I decided to write a *story*, because I wanted to show how a bad situation actually turned out for good. In a narrative the event itself would have been the important thing. In the story I wrote, what I learned about myself and other people was the important thing, and I used the events to illustrate that point.

That is not to say that all good stories have to hit the reader over the head with an Important Message. The purpose of many stories is simply to entertain, and that's a worthy goal, too. Even to entertain, though, a story must be carefully planned to have the effect you want it to have.

B. Story structure

Narrative is a well-related sequence of events, like lengths of lumber neatly laid out in a building supply store. **Story** is the same lumber, cut, fitted, and nailed together to build a house. Just as a house should have a plan before the builder begins, a story should have a **structure**. This is the basic structure of a story:

1. **Opening**. Usually just a paragraph, sometimes as brief as one sentence, to attract the reader and set the stage.
2. **Rising action**. Covers about one-half to three-fourths of the story. Shows actions leading up to the climax. Also can reveal character and show how the characters move the action.

3. **Climax**. One-fourth or less. The high point of the story, to which all previous action has led.

4. **Falling action**. One-fourth or less. Shows logical results of the climax, and concludes the story .

The profile of a story would look like this:

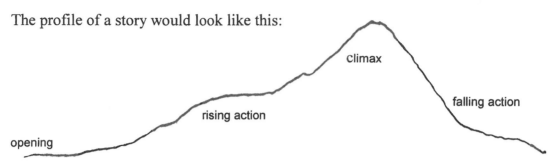

Notice that it takes a long time to build up to the climax, and only a short time to finish, just as it may take hours to climb a mountain, but only a few seconds to fall off. Usually a story starts out with all kinds of possibilities, a sense that anything could happen. But after the climax there are few surprises. Everything left over is **anti-climax**, and no reader wants to slog along through pages of conclusion after the suspense is gone.

Story structure is not just for fictional tales. Stories drawn from your own experience or historical fact can be, and often are, shaped to follow the same pattern. Fitting an actual experience to a pattern does not mean lying about it--it just means deciding what to leave out, what to tell, and how to tell it. This is the way that stories have been told for thousands of years, and no one has come up with an improvement on the basic formula. As an example, notice the comparison of two very old stories: "The Boy Who Cried Wolf," and "Cinderella."

OPENING	"Once upon a time, there lived a boy who watched the sheep for his village."	After her father dies, Cinderella is worked like a slave by her evil stepmother and her two ugly stepsisters.
RISING ACTION	1. The boy continually plays tricks on his countrymen by crying "Wolf!" when there is no wolf. 2. He is warned by his parents and village elders. 3. He persists in his silly game.	1. An invitation to the Prince's ball arrives. 2. Cinderella longs to go, but her family only laughs at her--meanwhile keeping her up night after night to sew their gowns. 3. On the big night, Cinderella's fairy godmother appears and creates a dress, coach and servants to take her to the ball--but she must leave before midnight, when the enchantment fades. 4. At the ball, the prince insists on dancing every dance with her. 5. At midnight she flees, leaving one slipper behind. 6. The prince determines to try the glass slipper on every lady's foot until he finds his lost love.
CLIMAX	A real wolf appears and the boy's warning is ignored.	Cinderella tries the glass slipper, and it fits.
FALLING ACTION	The boy is killed because no one listens to him. Don't let this happen to you!	She marries the prince and lives happily ever after.

TRY IT: Find a human interest article in the local newspaper. "Human interest" features tell about events of ordinary life, such as a rescued pet, a national award won by a local child, or former high school sweethearts meeting again after fifty years. Newspaper "stories" are not stories at all in the sense that I am using here, but with some thought a story could be made of the elements given. Make a list of the events related in the feature. Where's the climax? Underline it. What details lead to the climax, and which could be left out? What purpose (entertaining, moral, inspirational) could this story have? How could you structure the events to bring this out? Could anything be added, any details filled in?

Look back at the ski narrative on pages 64-65. The author wrote a lovely paragraph that includes action, description, and emotion. She creates the setting and describes events that build to a climax of sorts. But the paragraph can't be considered a story because there's one essential element missing: a sense of **conflict**.

The narratives you wrote in Section 6 may have rising action, climax and falling action. Some may have gone on for several pages. But without a central conflict they are not stories, no matter how long they are. Every novel you've ever read, every play, movie or TV show you've ever seen has at least one conflict. It may be between individuals (Jim Hawkins and Long John Silver in *Treasure Island,* for example). Or it may be between a character and his society (Romeo and Juliet against their feuding families), or one group against another (Aslan's forces vs. the crew of the White Witch in *The Lion, The Witch and The Wardrobe).* Quite often, the main conflict is between an individual and his own human failings--think of Pinocchio, in the Disney movie of that name.

Back to the ski narrative: if we wished to create a conflict, we could show how the heroine has been fighting all day--fighting the elements, the force of gravity, her equipment and her own discouragement. She recognizes and dislikes a tendency in herself to give up too easily, but this time she makes up her mind to see it through. The rising action would show her struggles, her tears, her temptation to call it quits. The climax could be the moment when she catches a glimmer of hope through one small success. *Or* the climax could come when she suffers her worst fall and faces her deepest discouragement--but determines to get up and try once more. One climax emphasizes hope, the other emphasizes will power. It's up to the author to decide just where the climax will come, depending on what he or she wants to say.

At the point of climax, the story turns a corner. The conflict is **resolved**. The narrative paragraph picturing that last downhill run would do very nicely (and almost literally) for falling action, as our heroine celebrates victory not just over the slope, but over her own discouragement. Here's how the narrative could be re-structured as a story:

```
Conflict:         Battling my own discouragement
Rising Action:    Long waits allow fear to build up
                  Seeing how fast my brother catches on (argggh!)
                  Skiing into that cute instructor (double argggh!)
                  Getting sore from falling down
                  Instructor: "lead with your mind, not your body"
                  My worst fall--is this the end?
```

```
Climax:          My first successful run
Falling Action:  This is fun!
                 "No way--I'm an expert!"
```

TRY IT: Look back at the narratives you wrote in Section 8 and choose the one you like best. I won't ask you to rewrite it as a story, but take a moment to *think* of it as a story. The events narrated will probably suggest some sort of conflict to you, such as, "My little brother's whining was getting on my nerves and threatened to ruin a beautiful day." How could the rising action be structured to spotlight that conflict? Locate the turning point, or **resolution**, when the conflict is settled one way or another. That's your climax. Write your possible story structure below:

Central Conflict: _____

_____

Rising Action:

1. _____

2. _____

3. _____

4. _____

Climax: _____

Falling action: _____

C. Me?! Write a story?!

You may have seen puzzles like the one below. If you colored every space that contains a dot, a word or picture will emerge. What is the word? (The puzzle is an illustration only--you are not required to color in this course.)

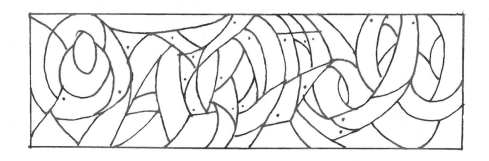

Just as you would color only the spaces with a dot in order to reveal the word, when you sit down to write you must include only those details and incidents that reveal your purpose. This is easier said than done, of course.

Suppose someone escorted you into a warehouse, parked you in front of a chunk of marble twice your size, and said, "We want a new statue for Millard Fillmore Memorial Park. Here's a mallet and chisel. Sculpt us a statue of Millard Fillmore." Chances are, you'd panic. You've never sculpted so much as a toothpick before; how can they expect you to turn out a statue of a man you've never seen using skills you never learned?

You may have the same feelings when you are asked to write a story. Where to begin? What to say? What to write about? By now you've learned that you have a lot of experiences to write about, but even so, it isn't easy to chip a good story out of the huge chunk of your experience. However, remember that you've already learned a lot about picking and choosing. When describing a person, you stay close to one overriding impression of that person. When narrating action you focus on one incident. In the description of a place you include only those details that communicate your strongest feelings about that place. In other words, you chip away all the "extra" material until one polished and shaped segment of your experience is expressed in words.

Think of something that happened to you: particularly, an incident that changed you in some way. Perhaps it was the moment you found the courage to stand up for something you believe in, or that time you realized you were being thoughtless. Perhaps you'll remember the family get-together that turned out to be more fun than you thought, or the "weird" neighbor you came to respect. It won't necessarily be the most exciting or scary thing that ever happened to you. Often it's the everyday occurrences that teach us the most--the events we don't appreciate until a little time gives us perspective.

As you probably guessed, you are about to write about that experience--as a story, not a narrative. Before writing a line, you need to think about how the story will be structured. On a clean sheet of notebook paper, write the central conflict: is it between you and another individual? you and yourself? your group against another group? Or does the conflict arise between other parties, with you as an observer or a go-between? All these or a combination of any are possible.

Once you've identified the conflict you can make your outline. Start with the climax; this will be the turning point where you were moved to action or understood something you hadn't recognized before. Where would you locate the climax in your story?

Write the climax on a line about halfway down the page, then list the events that led up to it. Here you'll have to think carefully, because you won't necessarily include everything that happened. What should be included are all the events that created the situation (conflict) and brought it to a head. Below the climax, list one or two results of it: the falling action. The items you list should form a logical progression.

Now you have an outline, a skeleton. The story you write will be the flesh on these bones. Before you get started, ask someone to read your skeleton--outline, I mean--and see if the progression makes sense. If this person is familiar with the event you plan to tell about, he or she may think of an important step you left out. Consider any suggestions, but the final decision about what goes into your story belongs to *you*.

You're ready to begin the most ambitious assignment in this book. Take a day off.

D. Getting off the ground

Which of these sentences would make the best opening for a story? Rate them from "4" for "most interesting" to "1" for "least interesting":

_____ "This is going to be the greatest vacation we ever had," Dad promised.

_____ I lay flat on the surfboard, tingling with anticipation as the next wave roared up behind me.

_____ As we packed our suitcases for Hawaii, I had no way of knowing how memorable this vacation was going to be.

_____ Once our family went to Hawaii for a summer vacation.

If you ranked the last sentence as the least interesting, I agree. Do *not*, at least this time, begin your story with the words "once," or "one day," "one time," "one summer," etc. This is not because such sentences are bad, but because they are too easy, and often too boring. The Opening sentence of a story is a tool used by the author to grab a reader's attention. Go for the grab!

One technique many authors use is to begin the story smack dab in the middle of the action, as in the second sentence above, or in these examples:

I gently turned the knob and eased the door open.

Stephanie leaned over me, glaring.

Others prefer a bit of introduction, to slide the reader into a time and place:

The summer I spent at my Grandma's in Maine seems almost magical to me now.

Still others begin with a hint of how the story will turn out:

After the garden party fiasco, I asked myself what evil spirit possessed me to take my little brother with me that day.

You get to decide which approach is best for your story. Just remember, the opening sentence should catch your readers' interest enough to make them want to read more. Write three or four opening sentences, then choose the one that makes the best attention-grabber.

You have a plan, an outline, and an opening sentence: you're on a roll! From here on your story will follow the rules for narrative writing, for the main difference between story and narrative is not style but structure. As you write, keep these guidelines in mind:

1. Use first person, at least this time. When you have more experience with story writing it will be fun to try different "persons" and points of view.
2. Explain any background the reader needs to know in a summary paragraph.
3. Stay focused on the events leading to the climax.
4. Use sensory details--tell what you saw, heard, touched and felt.
5. **Show, don't tell**. Don't explain that "Dad was upset," but show by Dad's actions and words how he felt. Use facial expressions, posture, and actions, as you did when describing people in section 4.
6. Use dialogue (back and forth conversation) at least once, along with single direct quotes.
7. Include some description of the place your story occurs, or, if the story involves more than one place, describe where the climax occurs. Description should not take more than three sentences.
8. Feel free to use figures of speech (especially simile and metaphor) as they occur to you-- but don't overdo it.

That's a lot to think about. Did you notice how story writing includes all the aspects of writing you've practiced in this book? (You may exclude poetry, but I think a little poetry works its way into all good writing.) Reviewing this list of guidelines now and than as you write will help you keep them in mind. It may help to refer to them if you get stuck. Don't try to write the entire story in one day, but don't let it drag out too long, either--you'll loose your train of thought. It's a good idea to indicate on your outline how much of the story you expect to write each day.

Now, get started. Length? As long as it takes to tell the story, from a few pages to twenty. Plan on at least four. Some authors start out writing short stories and end up with novels--the story just didn't quit! That's not likely to happen to you, but you may be surprised. If you get stuck, refer to the next section.

HOW TO DEAL WITH WRITERS' BLOCK

"Writers' block" is the dreaded affliction of wordsmiths who find their fountain of ideas drying up. If this happens to you, check out the following possibilities:

1. Perhaps you're just tired, and should put everything aside while you go have lunch or shoot some hoops or take a nap. Try not to stay away for more than twenty-four hours, though--the longer you're separated from your manuscript the harder it will be to get back into it.

2. You may have bogged down in too much description or too much dialogue or whatever. Check your outline again--have you taken a wrong turn? Perhaps you should not have started that explanation of why the coach said what he did or how Sally played that trick on Jason, because it took you away from the structure. Perhaps you should back up, cross out the last two or three paragraphs of the story and get back to your outline.

3. You may discover that the *outline* is wrong. As you work the story out in actual words and sentences, new insights may come to you and you may even realize that the climax wasn't where you thought. If that's the case, write out a new outline. It should take much less time than the first because now you have a clearer idea of where you're headed. With the road map corrected, you should enjoy easier motoring.

4. I hate to mention it, but perhaps you shouldn't be writing *this* story at all. It could be that you don't yet understand this particular experience well enough to make a story out of it. Save it for a narrative instead. Sit back, think of something else, and start over with a new outline. All that time was not wasted--you still got in lots of good writing practice.

When your story is complete, proofread and put it aside for a few days while you rest up for the revision job ahead.

Take at least two days to revise. First, read the whole story to get a sense of the flow and organization. If any obvious flaw jumps out at you in the first reading, make a quick note in the margin and keep reading to the end.

Now consider the overall structure. Does the action move smoothly to the climax? Did you notice any places where more detail would have helped? Perhaps some details should be left out because they slow down your momentum. What should you add? What should you take out? Does the falling action "tie up" all the loose ends? Rethink, rearrange, cross out, draw arrows, and think some more.

Once you feel satisfied that the story flows well and you can do no more with structure, revise the text as you are accustomed. Use the story guidelines on p. 83 and Revision Checklist #2 to remind you of all you need to watch for. Mark all changes and put the story aside again. Here's what a corrected draft might look like:

The minute I saw my brother's ^*red* shorts disappear into the

water of the lake, I knew my little joke had gone too far.

Until then,

^It was a beautiful day.. ~~Flowers~~ *Daffodils* were blooming and the

fresh breeze smelled good *like spring*, though it was ~~still early~~ *only the second Sat. in March*. Dad

took me and Jesse, my ~~little~~ *10-year-old* brother, to ~~the~~ *Mission* park for an

afternoon. Jesse is usually a pretty good kid, but he

wasn't having a good day. He lost his kite when the

decided the whole world was against him.

string broke and ~~started pouting.~~ When we stopped at the

snack bar, he even turned down an ice cream cone.

"I feel adventurous," Dad said.

~~Dad said he felt adventurous.~~ I knew he was trying to

cheer Jesse up, because soon he was renting a paddleboat.

Jesse loves paddleboats, so he perked up a little.

But not for long. Once we were in the middle of the lake,

he decided it wasn't fair that he didn't have any ice

cream. Dad explained patiently that Jesse himself had

turned down the ice cream when he had the chance, but

my little brother

still ~~he~~ whined to go back.

By now my good mood had turned sour. Since Jesse had

spoiled it for me, why shouldn't I get back at him? "Hey,

offering my cold, dripping

Jesse," I said, ~~as I offered my~~ cone. "You can have a lick

rocky road

of my ~~ice cream~~." Angrily he shook his head. "Come on,"

coaxed

I ~~said~~, "I haven't even touched this side." He leaned

jerked

toward the cone, but I ~~pulled~~ it back with a teasing

laugh.   Furious, he hurled himself at me--and missed.   He
flew
~~fell~~ over the side of the boat and *splashed* into the water.

"Jesse!" Dad yelled, and before I could say anything,

he had dived into the lake, too.   I knew I was in trouble

when both their dripping heads emerged from the water.

The look on Dad's face told me I'd be grounded for at

least a week.

We laugh about it now, but I've learned to treat bad

moods with kid gloves. *As my grandma says, "If you don't want a fire, don't strike a match."*

Some authors revise their work any number of times, but you can settle for twice unless you're a real perfectionist. Read your story once again (as well as you can maneuver around all the arrows, cross-outs and additions) and make any final changes. Copy or print out the story and draw illustrations if you're good at that kind of thing. Then get someone to read it. Get several people to read it. Your experiences should be shared!

You have now "graduated" from this course. Perhaps you are no more enthusiastic about writing than when you started, but let me share some of my hopes for you anyway.

I hope you will feel a little more confident now when you pick up a pencil or pen. I hope you will be encouraged to experiment with words and sentences, and perhaps even have fun doing it. I hope you learn how to communicate with words more effectively, so that when your grandmother reads your next Thank-you letter she'll almost feel like you're taking to her. I hope you start looking at the world around you in a new way, noticing things you never noticed before, making discoveries about yourself and others. Most of all, I hope you understand better how to communicate the experience given to *you,* and no one else.

APPENDICES

APPENDIX A: HOW TO PROOFREAD

The secret of proofreading is to train yourself to see only what's on the page in front of your eyes. This sounds easy, but isn't. Your brain thinks it knows what's on the page, and you will allow your eyes to skip over whole groups of words if you're not careful. Even if your eyes catch a mistake, your bossy brain may not let them "see" anything wrong.

The point to remember is that you can't glance over an assignment you've written and assume that you've caught every mistake. Most books are proofread several times by several readers before they're published, and even that does not guarantee a final copy with no errors.

However, here are a few tricks to encourage your brain to stay alert while your eyes are trying to do their job.

1. Read your paper out loud. This usually makes you slow down.

2. Hold a ruler or straight edge under each line as you read it.

3. Read the last sentence first, then the next-to-last sentence, then the sentence before that one, and so on all the way to the beginning.

4. If you can't seem to help reading too fast, use a pencil to point to each word.

You may want to vary these techniques. They will help, but remember that it's ultimately up to you to *look* at what you've written.

APPENDIX B: HOW TO REVISE

Your goal in **proofreading** was to catch spelling, punctuation and grammatical errors. In **revision** you must dig deeper and ask yourself some hard questions, all having to do with the purpose and quality of your work. The Big Question is: Did I say this as well as I could have?

As I mentioned before, nobody writes it right the first time. Occasionally you may sit down and whip out a story or assignment that seems inspired--but it will still need some minor revision, at least. Accept that, and aim for the best work you can do. Here are six steps to systematic revision:

1. After writing anything, let at least 24 hours pass before attempting a thorough revision.

2. When you are ready to read your work, try to distance yourself from it as much as possible. Imagine that you know *nothing* about the subject of the paper--you are ready to be informed.

3. Read through the piece in its entirety without stopping. If you see any obvious errors or problems, mark them quickly in the margins, then read on. You should try to get a feeling for the "flow," the overall structure. Some areas of your paper may seem weak--they need more detail, a little more explanation.   Other areas may seem over-involved or unnecessary. You may notice places where you repeated yourself or tried to cover too much ground in too small a space. The ending may seem abrupt, leaving you with an unsatisfied feeling, as if you had expected more and didn't get it. If any of these seems to be a problem, note them *quickly* with a check or question mark or a secret symbol of your own (as long as you know what it means).

4. After the first reading, take a moment to review objectives on the revision checklist. With these goals firmly in mind, read your paper again, slowly and carefully this time. In the first reading you looked at the material as a whole; now you will watch for specifics. Cross out unnecessary words and phrases; make substitutions for weak nouns, verbs, or modifiers; rearrange or rewrite sentences to make them more forceful; add background information where needed to help the reader understand; add detail to help the reader "see."

5. Long narratives or stories (three pages or more) should be revised twice. After the first revision, set it aside for another 24 hours. If you have a word processor, enter the changes you made during the first revision and print it out. This gives you a clean copy to work with. For the second revision follow the same procedure, reading once for overall structure and content, again for word choice and sentence structure.

6. Your paper should look like a mess by now--if it doesn't, something's wrong! Copying this should be a pleasure. Work slowly, write carefully and turn in your assignment with the well-earned satisfaction of having done your very best.

REVISION CHECKLIST #1

1. Did you include several specific details?
2. Are there any nouns that could be made more concrete?
3. Should any neutral verbs be made stronger?
4. Are sentences nicely varied in length and structure?
5. Are there any colloquialisms outside a direct quote? (See Caveat #2 on p. 17.)

REVISION CHECKLIST #2

1. Do you see any unnecessary words or phrases, such as adverbs where a strong verb would be more effective, modifiers that could be done without (especially qualifiers like "really," "very," "little," etc.), meaningless or padded phrases ("at this point in time," "all in all," "in any case," etc.)?
2. Do you hear any "echoes"--repeated words or phrases?
3. Does the opening sentence attract attention?
4. Does the closing paragraph or sentence make a strong conclusion, or is it vague and wishy-washy?
5. Are *all* general statements supported by concrete details?
6. Do all quotes and dialogue add something to the narrative (provide information, advance story, or reveal character)?
7. Does the writing stay focused? Should any paragraphs or sentences be left out because they have little to do with the subject of your description or story?

Remember, a revised draft should look like a mess! Here's an example of the draft I made for the fourth paragraph on page 53, with corrections.

APPENDIX C: VERB LIST

This list is intended only to give you an idea of how many ways there are to do these basic activities. Add your own!

Verbs of Expression		Verbs of Motion	
Speech:	Sight:	stride	pace
snap	leer	march	trudge
growl	peep	lumber	stumble
sneer	spy	amble	hobble
sniff	peer	limp	pace
chatter	squint	glide	march
whisper	glare	saunter	dart
mumble	glance	stroll	dash
murmur	scowl	skip	gallop
mutter	gaze	strut	tear
drawl	ogle	swagger	bolt
recite	scan	sweep	leap
pronounce	behold	lope	scurry
chant			
drone	_____	_____	_____
prattle			
gush	_____	_____	_____
stammer			
stutter	_____	_____	_____
sputter			
shriek	_____	_____	_____
howl			
holler	**Verbs of**	**Verbs of**	
bawl	**Repose**	**contact**	
cheer	droop	shove	kiss
hiss	slouch	heave	stroke
snarl	stall	crash	massage
giggle	stoop	ram	slap
wail	pose	collide	shoulder
sob	straddle	graze	
scold	lounge	lap	
	crouch	nudge	_____
_____	cower	press	
	cringe	slam	_____
_____	squat	thump	
	perch	grope	_____
_____	roost	tap	
	nestle	finger	_____
_____		paw	
	_____	brush	
_____	_____	caress	_____

APPENDIX D: EXAMPLES

Poems:

1.   Fall smells like hot apple cider.
       Fall tastes like a Thanksgiving turkey.
       Fall looks like red, orange, and yellow leaves, spinning to the ground.

       In fall I can hear geese flying south for the winter.
       In fall I can feel crisp brown leaves crunching beneath my feet.

2. I like harvest time.

Harvest time is crisp, clear and cool
Like the early morning of a spring day.
The brightest red and yellow of harvest time
      are like a quivering fire.

The wind is like a whistling train
      Or sometimes a roaring hurricane,
And from a distance the shine of harvest time
      Is like the shine of gold.

The bare trees tower high above me
      Like giant skyscrapers,
And the leaves under my feet crackle
      Like a roaring fire.
The blasts of wind fetch the leaves like an invisible hand.

And by the way, what do you think of fall?

3.

             Remembering
        the time of year I like best:
          its name is spring.

     I see all the plants and trees come to life
         and everything is new.
     I feel the warm, sweet-smelling breeze
         blow around me.

       I listen to the birds
     chirping and building their nests.
        It reminds me
    of all the good times I've had in my life.

4. Soccer--
running into the wind,
spying an opponent on my left
getting plowed over as I dribble the ball.
Smelling the grass,
Tasting the dirt,
Hearing the referee's shrill whistle.

Getting up,
Taking a free kick,
Rocketing the ball to a teammate.

Kicking the ball through a cage of legs,
Running towards the goal
As I score for my team!

Huddling with the coach,
Making plans,
Picking positions,
Yawning on the benches,
Warming the seat for a teammate.

Winning the game!
(some things never change),
walking out to the car.

Going home now,
Taking a shower,
Glancing at the calendar:
More practice tomorrow.
Soccer.

5. Before dawn, a spooky-looking piece of sky
      Creeps over the hills
            And settles down in the valleys.
                  Like a ghost, it sneaks between the trees.
            And gives everything a cold, damp feeling.
      Silently it came, and silently it slides away,
   Leaving no trace that it had ever been there.

6.   BLACK
            Looks like the dark of a moonless night,
            Sounds like someone sneaking up on you,
            Smells like hot tar,
            Tastes like overripe berries,
            Feels like a soft leather jacket.

Descriptions:

7.   It's dark outside. Inside I'm sitting at a desk, with a gray computer monitor staring at me. I hear the soft humming of computers and the loud crack of the printer. My hand is resting on smooth wood. I smell cigarette smoke and the crisp scent of new paper. Directly in front of me are boxes stuffed with disks. A radio is playing softly in my right ear and at my left is a stack of papers packed into folders. Arghhhh, this place makes me tired.

8.   You walk past some brown, half-dead prickly bushes, then up the gray concrete steps to the cold black door you always need to push to get open. As you step in, the sound of babies cooing and the low murmur of the TV is usually in the background. When you walk in it looks as though someone were walking toward you, then you realize it is just your reflection in the hall mirror. You sit down in the living room, and feel like you're about to sink right through the soft, dark couch.
       Across from the living room are double doors, which let in the soft, warm sunshine. The atmosphere at my friend's house, any time of day, is relaxing and comfortable.

9.   The sun is setting. I look around in this eerie place and see brown and white bottles, drawers full of papers, sick-looking people, barred windows. I'm surrounded by shelves with bottles on them. Strange sounds meet my ears: the continuous scrape of a knife across a tray, a phone ringing, a printer squealing, and a jangling bell as the cash register opens. I feel the strength of the soft, squishy cotton struggling to hold on to the neck of the bottle. I give it a yank and it releases its grip, soars through the air and lands in the trash can.
       Working at my dad's pharmacy can be an interesting experience.

10.   My friend is wearing a brown, black and white coat with matching white socks. She is medium-built and not very tall. It looks like she is posing for a picture as she stares out the window. I can tell by the way her tail wags that she is eager for something to happen. She is feeling good. Something like this might be going through her mind as the water meter man crosses the lawn: "You trespasser." She is on a windowsill about one foot wide with the autumn sun pouring around her. Looking out the window, she says, "Grrrrr!"

REVIEW QUIZ #1

I. In the paragraphs below, replace each underlined word with a more concrete noun, and conclude with a direct quote. What the characters say will depend on the nouns you select.

As the <u>boat</u> moved closer, two <u>men</u> jumped from the deck onto the <u>ground</u>. One pulled <u>something</u> from under his coat. The other tipped his <u>hat</u> at some girls standing nearby and said, "_____

_____."

The <u>car</u> screeched to a stop. The doors on both sides popped open and <u>people</u> started piling out. Laughing and talking loudly, they made their way toward the <u>building</u>, but were blocked by a <u>man</u> at the door, who shouted, "_____

_____."

II. Change the verbs in these sentences to reflect how the character is feeling.

1. Tom <u>ran</u> to me. "What do you think you're doing?" he <u>said</u>.

2. The teacher <u>walked</u> into the classroom.

3. The fans <u>yelled</u> when the referee made his call.

4. Tim <u>stood</u> in the doorway, his hands in his pockets.

5. Jasmine <u>set</u> her books on the table.

III. In the dialogue below, write one descriptive adjective to substitute for each underlined word.

A: Hi. Did you have a <u>nice</u> time at the party?

B: Great! The Johnsons are the <u>nicest</u> family.

A: They have a <u>nice</u> house, I hear.

B: Yes, but they're not snobs. Mrs. Johnson was so <u>nice</u> to me.

A: Really? That's nice.

IV. Rewrite each sentence, adding two prepositional phrases. One of the phrases should tell when, where, or how; the other should tell something about the subject. If you have trouble thinking of phrases, check the list of prepositions on page 19.

1. The twins played a game.

_____

_____

_____

2. The boys thanked Mr. Hendrickson.

_____

_____

_____

3. The mothers screamed.

_____

_____

_____

V. You will find no personal pronouns in the paragraph below--no wonder it reads so awkwardly. Eliminate as many "Jims" and "Tims" as possible and substitute a pronoun or an appropriate noun (such as "the brothers").

Tim and Jim attended Tim's and Jim's sister Christine's ballet recital at Truman High School on Saturday. Before long, Jim and Tim were so bored that when Tim asked to go get a drink, Jim slipped out with Tim. Jim and Tim wandered the school, finally ending up in a room where lots of girls were standing around in costume. Jim and Tim were backstage, and Christine's class was going on! Jim and Tim sneaked onstage with the class and were performing arabesques when the teacher pulled Jim and Tim off.

REVIEW QUIZ #2

I. Each of these sentences can be improved. Decide what the problem is: passive voice, a weak opening, colorless verbs or nouns, etc., then rewrite.

1. Jim hit the ball very hard.

_____

2. Huge spending bills are passed every week by Congress.

_____

3. We need people to work for this cause.

_____

4. when Ty and Hal were at baseball practice, he broke his wrist.

_____

5. There is a lilac bush on the corner where you should turn.

_____

6. Centerville Library has a great selection of children's books.

_____

7. The computer was fixed by Office Stop.

_____

8. The telephone rang.

_____

9. Mr. Brown ate his breakfast.

_____

10. Gwendolyn was terrified by that scary movie.

_____

11. There is life where there is hope.

_____

II. Add descriptive adjectives and prepositional phrases, change nouns and verbs and rewrite sentences (especially the first and last sentences) to make this paragraph more interesting.

It was a hot summer day. Howard and I took our boat to the water. We set the boat in the water. We climbed on. We floated for a while. Howard saw a flat brown shell coming toward us. Then a head stuck up out of it. "It's a snapping turtle!" Howard said. We pretended it was an alien space craft and shot at it with sticks until it went away. We had fun.

III. Rewrite these sentences so they don't start with "I":

1. I see sparkling waves on the ocean.

_____

2. I hear seagulls crying.

_____

3. I smell fish in the air.

_____

4. I feel the wet grainy sand under my toes.

_____

5. I taste the Popsicle I bought from the ice cream wagon.

_____

REVIEW QUIZ #3

I. Write a sense poem about white, showing how it looks, sounds, smells, tastes, and feels.

_____

_____

_____

_____

_____

II. Choose *one* of these three objects, and write a personification of it as it does its work.

   A vacuum cleaner   A fax machine   A garbage disposal

_____

_____

_____

III. On a separate sheet of paper, rewrite these paragraphs to include more sensory detail: add at least three sense impressions per paragraph and try to include one simile or one metaphor in each. (Such as "In the west, the sky gathers into a big black frown," or "The clown towered over me like a toy grown to nightmare size.")

> 1. I love summer rainstorms. The first thing I notice is dark clouds gathering on the horizon, usually in the west. Before long I can feel a wind coming from that direction that cools things off. Sometimes the clouds move in very fast, and everybody runs around to pick up things they don't want to get wet. Then big, fat raindrops fall-- sometimes hail, which is even more exciting. After the storm moves through everything looks cleaner.

> 2. One of the scariest memories of my childhood is a birthday party at Captain Jack's Pizza Parlor. I was only five, and wasn't used to all the noise and flashing lights from the arcade and the kiddie rides. My mother kept urging me to join the fun, but I was too overwhelmed. Then a clown appeared, and came right over to me and tried to get me involved. I'm sure he meant well, but he was so big and noisy I was terrified! My mother took me home after that.

REVIEW QUIZ # 4

I. Rewrite these sentences to *show*, not just *tell*. It will probably help to invent a setting for each, and you may add a direct quote or an additional sentence.

1. He looks happy and pleased.

_____

_____

2. The room was messy.

_____

_____

3. I could tell she was very disappointed.

_____

_____

4. I feel contented and peaceful.

_____

_____

5. He walked toward me in a determined manner.

_____

_____

II. On a separate sheet of paper, rewrite the first paragraph to show Sarah's personality by what she does. Rewrite the second to show the action, rather than just describing it. Feel free to add direct quotes, dialogue, or any details that seem appropriate.

1. The thing I like best about my friend Sarah is that she's so warm and understanding. I feel that I can tell her anything and she wouldn't get mad. When I call her on the phone she always sounds like she's glad to hear from me. I'm blessed to have a friend like that.

2. Hank knocked on the door of the deserted warehouse but there didn't seem to be anyone there. He stepped inside, and noticed right away that something was wrong. There was an odd smell that seemed to come from the corner on his right. He looked that way, but didn't see anything.